WILLIAMS-SONOMA

NEW ORLEANS

AUTHENTIC RECIPES CELEBRATING THE FOODS OF THE WORLD

Recipes and Text
CONSTANCE SNOW

Scenic and Recipe Photographs
FRANCESCA YORKE

Recipe Photographs
QUENTIN BACON

General Editor
CHUCK WILLIAMS

Oxmoor
House®

CONTENTS

RECIPES

APPETIZERS AND FIRST COURSES

SOUPS AND GUMBOS

MAIN COURSES

VEGETABLES AND SIDES

DESSERTS AND SWEETS

INTRODUCTION

Say "New Orleans" and most people immediately think of the food—hot beignets and café au lait, fragrant bowls of gumbo and crawfish bisque, heaps of spicy boiled crabs on newspaper-lined tables, and elegant French Creole feasts in grand old restaurants that serve dinner with a view to the past.

CULINARY HISTORY

The distinctive cuisine of Louisiana has slowly evolved over the last three hundred years. Today, it is a rich and complex combination of flavors stirred up by Native Americans, French and Spanish colonists, African and Caribbean slaves, and immigrants from Germany, Italy, Ireland, Croatia, and parts of Asia. The cultural center of New Orleans flourished around the mouth of the Mississippi River, a major port of entry for fine European goods and exotic produce from Central and South America. Riverboats carried these luxuries to the rest of the nation, and New Orleans became known as a retreat for haute cuisine and high living during the mid-nineteenth century, earning a reputation for civilized overindulgence and genial carnality that continues to this day.

The city's oldest restaurant is Antoine's, a grand French Quarter landmark with its maze of fifteen dining rooms enriched by dark woods, potted palms, and polished chandeliers. Since Antoine Alciatore first opened his doors in 1840, the formally clad staff has welcomed the world's luminaries,

from Count Albrecht von Bismarck to Mick Jagger. The second-oldest restaurant is Tujague's, also in the French Quarter, established in 1856 and named for Madame Marie Abadie Tujague, whose lavish meals launched the venerable restaurant and attracted an international clientele that eventually included several American presidents and hundreds of other notables. Even native New Orleanians might be surprised to learn that their third-oldest eatery is the casual Bruning's Sea Food Restaurant, established by German immigrant Theodor Bruning in 1859. (The original lakefront structure was badly damaged by Hurricane Georges in 1998, but the operation continues in new quarters next door.) Bustling sidewalk Café du Monde, a landmark on Jackson Square, has served its famous café au lait and beignets since the 1860s.

Many of the most fashionable newer restaurants have historical connections as well. Tennessee Williams completed work on *A Streetcar Named Desire* in the courtyard and rear apartment of what is now The Bistro

at Maison de Ville in the French Quarter. Just a few blocks away, chic Peristyle, which turns out exceptional, locally inspired French cuisine, overlooks the old Congo Square (believed by many to be the birthplace of jazz), where slaves gathered on Sundays to make music. The 1860 building currently inhabited by Ralph's on the Park was once a notorious coffeehouse, the meeting ground for ladies of the evening and their gentlemen friends, and the traditional spot to steady the nerves with brandy-laced caffeine after taking aim under the dueling oaks of City Park.

For a fascinating glimpse into the past, the Historic New Orleans Collection in the French Quarter maintains extensive files of early menus and photographs from local restaurants. Although not on display, the documents are part of the facility's archives at the Williams Research Center on Chartres Street, a mouthwatering record of the evolution of Creole and Cajun cuisine.

One of many misconceptions about Louisiana is that everyone who lives here is a Cajun, an image promoted by Hollywood

movies in which the citizens of New Orleans speak with broad French accents that would sound preposterous in the thickest backwater swamps. Actually, the culture—and cuisine—of south Louisiana can be divided into two broad categories. The Cajuns of the southwestern bayous and prairies are descended from French Acadians, peaceful country people that populated maritime Canada for more than one hundred years before the English drove them out in 1755. They first arrived in Louisiana during the eighteenth century, and their rustic and hearty cooking has roots that reach back to provincial France.

The city of New Orleans was settled in the early eighteenth century by Creoles, colonial offspring of European parents. Their kitchens have always turned out cosmopolitan fare for city people, based on the formal traditions of France and Spain but well seasoned by generations of African and Caribbean cooks. The classic French cuisine and zesty Spanish tomato sauces of Creole cooks are enlivened by tropical spices and fresh Gulf seafood.

Most people still associate New Orleans with its Gallic roots, but "the Paris of the Americas" was flooded during the nineteenth century by a wave of industrious Italian and Irish refugees, contemporaries of those who settled Brooklyn, Boston, and other port cities.

Among the countless Italian contributions to the local cuisine and culture are Central Grocery—famous for its muffuletta sandwich —and the Monteleone Hotel, both in the French Quarter, and Angelo Brocato's Ice Cream and Confectionery in Mid-City, plus a long tradition of no-nonsense cooking and no-frills service at dozens of neighborhood restaurants, famous for crisp fried seafood and old Sicilian standards draped in thick red sauces. Local Italian American families have worked as truck farmers for generations, supplying produce for chefs and markets.

Ireland gave New Orleans several historic watering holes, such as Molly's at the Market, Parasol's, and Pat O'Brien's, as well as the talented and influential Brennan family, since 1946 the creators of a stellar collection of the

city's top restaurants and a growing network of spin-offs around the country.

More recently the Keswani family has given spice-loving Louisiana and its Indian community a taste for exotic fine dining at Taj Mahal and Nirvana. Every neighborhood has at least one Chinese restaurant, and most also support a sushi bar (sometimes featuring such sacrileges as deep-fried sushi and all-you-can-eat sushi buffets, concessions to the prevailing local appetites). A huge influx of Vietnamese refugees during the 1980s added new workers to the commercial fishing industry, along with intriguing new foods that fit right into the ever-evolving Creole cuisine, such as grilled shrimp (prawn) cakes on sugarcane skewers, Asian-style stuffed crabs, pâtés, and hearty beef stews. "Vietnamese po-boys," dressed with marinated daikon, cucumber, carrots, and hot-pepper sauce, are a popular street food from Saigon and Hanoi. The bread and homemade mayonnaise used to make them are authentically French, holdovers from years of Gallic occupation in Vietnam.

CONTEMPORARY CUISINE

French Louisiana's Cajuns and Creoles began as two distinct communities, but cultural crossovers have always existed, especially in the kitchen. More fusion heated up the scene in the '80s and '90s, when a new generation of chefs added global flavors and popularized Louisiana cooking around the world.

Louisiana chefs have been a major force on the national scene for generations, none more so than the author of the definitive regional cookbook, *Chef Paul Prudhomme's Louisiana Kitchen.* Prudhomme's 1984 best-seller popularized his native Cajun cooking, a lifelong campaign that continues to be supported by his other books, television programs, licensed products, and French Quarter restaurant, K-Paul's Louisiana Kitchen. Emeril Lagasse may be best known as a star of the Food Network and king of a national restaurant domain, but he is also one of the earliest and best-regarded masters of contemporary Creole cuisine, drawing on a foundation of classical training in the kitchens of Paris, Lyons, Boston, and New York.

Contemporary Creole

It's neither easy nor fair to group the wide range of fashionable newer bistros under a single heading, but for the sake of quick reference in restaurant guides, they have come to be characterized as "contemporary Creole." It's actually a good term to describe the latest practitioners of an old culinary art, and although some of their innovations are viewed with alarm by preservationists of classic New Orleans cuisine, they are definitely part of a natural progression. Creole cookery is, by its very nature, a blend of many ethnic influences built up over successive generations, a constant evolution of flavors

and techniques that didn't end when Antoine's printed its first menu in 1840. In fact, a great many contemporary chefs and home cooks are keeping alive the most important tenets of the Creole kitchen.

Rule one: Make the most of seasonal homegrown ingredients. The best menus place an emphasis on regional foods, including seasonal produce and fresh herbs from Louisiana growers, handcrafted cheeses, free-range fowl, wild game, and the freshest Gulf fish and seafood. The best cooks seek out quirky local ingredients, such as squash blossoms, dewberries, mirlitons, muscadine grapes, and mayhaws.

Rule two: Start from scratch. From stocks to sausages, infused vinegars to ice creams, every element of a given dish begins in house, if at all possible. Emeril even makes his own Worcestershire sauce.

Rule three: Build on the old ways. Playful tweaks preserve the essence of beloved comfort foods while renovating them for enlightened tastes. A platter of cured duck might be edged with sweet potato–pecan ravioli. Raw oysters are slipped into shot glasses with a piquant chaser to make oyster shooters. Chopped fennel and Herbsaint liqueur (page 34) add a trace of anise flavor to crab stew. Smashed red potatoes are spiked with horseradish or green (spring) onions. Bread pudding is decked with white chocolate and dried cherries.

Rule four: When new people move into town, invite them to the table. Fresh flavors can only enrich the melting pot. Recent arrivals include crawfish spring rolls, shrimp (prawn) po-boys with wasabi mayonnaise, and grilled oysters with crisp Italian pancetta.

The Big Easy Diet

If only the doctors would tell us what we want to hear: Consume plenty of sugar, salt, and caffeine. Lean meats and fish should be fried or smothered in hollandaise. Drink six to eight glasses of beer daily. And never skip dessert. We could call it The Big Easy Diet.

A memorable 1970s-era cartoon by local artist Bunny Matthews shows a portly old gent, proclaiming to his dining companion, "It ain't da seafood dat makes ya fat. It's da batta." New Orleans has been proclaimed America's fattest city in more than one survey, and indeed it can be hard to resist the temptations that await around every corner— and as for exercise, well, it's just too hot. The low-carb Sugar Busters diet was created by a team of local doctors in the 1990s, and it has been embraced by restaurants and their patrons who are loathe to give up the béarnaise. Unfortunately, it has also inspired more than a few silly (and unlicensed) Sugar Buster Specials, such as platters of deep-fried seafood breaded with whole-wheat (wholemeal) flour and served with a side of sweet potato fries.

Dining at Home

Louisiana cuisine may be best known and loved for its wild abandon, but it also shares many healthful basics with the traditional Mediterranean diet. Like their forebears in France, Spain, and Italy, local families stock their kitchens with fresh tomatoes and homemade tomato sauces, homegrown vegetables, beans, greens, rice, pasta, cornmeal, olives, and olive oil. Younger cooks have also learned to replace much of the traditional pork fat and butter with lighter peanut or canola oil. Even though grand-mère would have been horrified, several brands of fat-free "dry roux" (browned flour) are now sold in jars, ready to add instant body and nutty flavor to étouffées and gumbos.

The Creole Trinity

Onions, bell peppers (capsicums), and celery are known as the Creole trinity, a trio of aromatics that seasons countless Louisiana soups, stews, sautés, roasts, and even other vegetables. Like its ancestors, the French mirepoix, Spanish sofrito, and Italian sofritto, the surprisingly versatile trinity is essential to the regional cuisine. Garlic makes it a quartet, always supporting the other aromatics in gumbos, courtbouillons, red beans, and other slow-pot recipes. The ubiquitous bay leaves and thyme are also derived from French Mediterranean roots.

Finally, pepper has its place, but it is used in moderate amounts—nowhere near the level in overpowering "Cajun" specialties concocted by many of the commercial packagers and chain restaurants. Louisianians do love their pepper, but they like to taste the food, as well.

DINING OUT

New Orleans cognoscenti compete for the favored tables at Galatoire's, and enjoy being served by their own regular waiters at Antoine's, but they also love to push up their sleeves at po-boy counters and crab shacks. Here, a knowledge of exquisite dives is just as important as keeping up with the trendiest bistros.

An opulent breakfast at The Court of Two Sisters or Brennan's is fine for a special occasion, but even the simplest morning meal in Louisiana can be a feast. If you find yourself in one of the small towns near New Orleans around breakfast time, seek out the café nearest the courthouse, the one full of plump lawyers and sheriff's deputies. In the city itself, head to The Old Coffee Pot in the French Quarter, Camellia Grill or Bluebird Cafe Uptown, or the coffee shop in any of the city's grand hotels. Breakfast at the popular Mother's restaurant in the Central Business District, where you can order creamy grits or hot biscuits with either "debris" (beef gravy dense with shreds from the carved roast) or burnt sugary end pieces of "black ham," is a Deep South splurge.

For lunch or dinner, the casual and funky old institutions known as "neighborhood restaurants" attract a wildly mixed crowd of bluebloods and blue collars. Slow-pot cooking turns out platters of creamy red beans and rice, smothered chicken, hearty seafood gumbo, rich duck étouffée, and other home-style Louisiana standards. Roast beef po-boys drip mayonnaise and gravy. The menus are heavy on comfort food, light on the wallet, drawing crowds to Liuzza's or Mandina's in Mid-City, Domilise's or Franky and Johnny's Uptown, R&O in Bucktown, or Fiorella's in the Quarter. In outlying areas, look for the parking lot with the most trucks.

A New Variety

Not so long ago, diners throughout New Orleans were likely to encounter well-meaning but unschooled answers to the question, "Do you have anything for vegetarians?" Among the recommendations were catfish or potato po-boys (stuffed with French fries drenched in beef gravy). A waiter might respond "the beans just have a little ham in them, and you can pick out the sausage." Now, even the old-school restaurants often have at least one meatless main dish, usually some variation on the meatlike portobello mushroom. But great vegetarian cuisine can be found on the menu at Lulu's in the French Quarter and Back to the Garden in the Central Business District.

Vietnamese, Thai, Japanese, Middle Eastern, Indian, and Cuban restaurants have proliferated in recent years and are now among some of the best and most popular eateries in the city. You'll find many of them located in the Uptown university area, Mid-City, Faubourg Marigny, and Old Metairie.

Good Connections

It could be argued that the modern age of fine dining in New Orleans began in 1946, when Owen Brennan launched the operation that would eventually become Brennan's French Restaurant on Royal Street. His sister, the formidable Ella Brennan, took charge after his death, expanding the family holdings to

include the Garden District landmark Commander's Palace (established by Emile Commander in 1880). The next generation of "Brennan cousins" now operates several of the city's most fashionable and highly regarded restaurants, including Bacco, Mr. B's Bistro, Palace Café, Dickie Brennan's Steakhouse, Ralph Brennan's Red Fish Grill, Ralph's on the Park, and Café Adelaide. Owen Brennan's sons and grandchildren remain at the helm of the original restaurant located in the French Quarter.

Meanwhile, Commander's Palace also helped launch the international career of former executive chef Paul Prudhomme, the Opelousas-born superstar who put Cajun cooking on the map. Frank Brigtsen, who apprenticed under Paul Prudhomme at Commander's, then followed his mentor to K-Paul's Louisiana Kitchen in the French Quarter, before opening his own Uptown restaurant, the multiple-award-winning Brigtsen's. Other Prudhomme protégés include Greg and Mary Sonnier, owners of the critically acclaimed Gabrielle Restaurant near City Park. All are enthusiastic supporters of regional products and growers, preserving the best of Creole and Cajun cooking.

Emeril Lagasse succeeded Prudhomme in the top job at Commander's Palace before becoming a TV phenomenon. In New Orleans alone, Lagasse's empire encompasses the original Emeril's in the Warehouse-Arts District, Nola in the French Quarter, and an elegant restoration of the century-old Delmonico Restaurant and Bar in the Garden District.

Both Lagasse and Brigtsen have been named Best Chef in the Southeast by the James Beard Foundation, an honor shared by Susan Spicer, who is building quite an empire herself. After winning raves at the small Bistro at Maison de Ville, Spicer opened her own French Quarter restaurant, Bayona, serving self-styled New World cuisine in a peaceful two-hundred-year-old cottage with garden decor. Two chic and modern spin-offs, Herbsaint and Cobalt, are both located on the St. Charles Avenue streetcar line.

Dinner Music

From festivals to funerals, food and music are inextricably linked in New Orleans. Snug Harbor Jazz Bistro in Faubourg Marigny is a pleasantly funky home base for world-class contemporary performers like pianist Ellis Marsalis (father of Wynton and Branford) and vocalist Charmaine Neville. If you'd rather avoid the lines and hard benches at the renowned Preservation Hall in the French Quarter, watch the same traditional jazz legends play at nearby Palm Court Jazz Café, where you can relax at a private table with good food and drinks. Food and music are earthy and filling at Tipitina's and House of Blues in the French Quarter or The Praline Connection in the Warehouse-Arts District, home of the gospel brunch. Also in the Warehouse District is Mulate's, an offshoot of the famed Cajun Country roadhouse, featuring foot-stomping zydeco. Young brass bands draw serious fans to Donna's Bar & Grill and Funky Butt, a couple of noisy neighbors on the seedier outskirts of the French Quarter.

Taylor's Happy Oaks Farm 4th Generation
Homemade Salad Dressings

Creole Tomato Salad Dressing: $ 6.00 per pint.
Ingredients: Farm fresh tomatoes, Sugar free mayonnaise, garlic & spices. Refrigerate. Lasts 4 to 6 weeks. Sugar free & no added salt.

Bleu Cheese Salad Dressing: $ 6.00 per pint.
Ingredients: Sugar free mayonnaise, garlic, bleu cheese & spices. Refrigerate. Lasts 4 to 6 weeks. Sugar free & no added salt.

Spinach Vinaigrette Salad Dressing: $ 7.00 per jar.
Ingredients: Extra virgin olive oil, homegrown raw baby spinach, white cider vinegar, garlic & spices. Refrigerate. Lasts 4 to 6 weeks in refrigerator. Sugar free & no added salt.

Homemade Salsa: $ 5.00 per pint.
Ingredients: Homegrown tomatoes, yellow onions, cilantro & spices. Refrigerate after opening. Sugar free. Lasts 1 to 2 weeks after opening.

SUPPORT YOUR FARMER'S MARKET—BUY FRESH!

MARKETS

The historic French Market is the oldest continuously operating outdoor market in the United States, but it is the exuberant Crescent City Farmers' Market that has revitalized the ancient custom of shopping outdoors with a handbasket, providing a fresh new outlet for New Orleans chefs and home cooks.

Even with today's superstores, most neighborhoods still depend on a small produce stand or a truck that is always stationed at a certain corner, purveyors of ripe Creole tomatoes, corn, strawberries, melons, navel oranges, and other seasonal vegetables and fruits. It's not uncommon to see a fisherman parked on the side of a road selling shrimp (prawns) from big ice chests on the tailgate of his pickup, cutting out the middleman.

Crescent City Farmers' Market

When Jim Core first began trucking produce into New Orleans from his farm in Folsom, Louisiana, he was wary about doing business in the big city. He told Richard McCarthy, director of Crescent City Farmers' Market, that he had even considered bringing along a shotgun. Then Core nearly lost his foot in a farming accident, "and suddenly the community boundaries shifted," McCarthy recalled. Chefs from some of the area's most sophisticated restaurants, who had come to depend on Core's homegrown seasonal vegetables, cooked at a benefit to help pay for his surgery. On the menu were dishes from Artesia, Bayona, Commander's Palace, Brigtsen's, and Peristyle—all this fuss for a country guy who still works his fields with a horse-drawn plow.

A commitment to tradition and properly nurtured ingredients has created a strong bond between regional growers and serious cooks, and this movement has grown steadily in Louisiana since the late 1970s. It took off in 1995 with the opening of the Crescent City Farmers' Market. The market began as a regular Saturday morning "block party" in the Warehouse-Arts District, an opportunity for residents of the urban neighborhood to purchase homegrown seasonal fruits and vegetables, cut flowers, bedding plants, breads, preserves, strawberry wine, fresh pastas, and other handcrafted foods. Supported by Loyola University and the nonprofit ECOnomics Institute, the community market has expanded to include seafood and dairy vendors. It has also grown to include the Tuesday morning market at Uptown Square, Wednesday mornings in the French Market, and Thursday afternoons at the American Can Company in Mid-City. Cooking demonstrations (and samples) from local chefs draw crowds every Saturday at 10 A.M. According to McCarthy, "Our motto is, 'It's never too early to start the day with garlic.'"

French Market

At the other end of the local timeline, the colonnaded structure of the historic French Market, located in the French Quarter, has been reconstructed many times since the 1790s, but the open-air operation still survives, despite centuries of floods, fires, and hurricanes. The original complex housed the cavernous Halles des Boucheries

(Butchers Market) and the adjoining Halles des Legumes (Produce Market). Today the ever-diminishing twenty-four-hour produce stands are squeezed among booths peddling seafood packed for shipping, Cajun and Creole products, hot sauces, and other tourist-oriented merchandise. Still, it's a fun ramble, especially the jumbled flea market.

In its glory days, the old French Market was a wild and colorful scene. Servants and housewives, out with their kitchen baskets, wove among fur traders, Native Americans, traveling peddlers, buccaneers, and barge-men. Besides caged fowl and mounds of produce, stalls were filled with whatever cargo had arrived on the nearby wharves, from imported linens to tropical birds. Crowds gathered to watch dentists who operated in public, sans anesthesia, although they did employ brass bands to drown out the screams.

Vietnamese Market

The Vietnamese community of eastern New Orleans meets every Saturday morning for an outdoor market that is crowded into the courtyard of a faded strip mall, just across the bayou from the intersection of Chef Menteur Highway and Paris Road. Dozens of neighborhood gardeners set up tables and blankets spread with exotic fruits, vegetables, and homemade treats. Fresh herbs (chives, basil, mint) are offered by the fistful at a fraction of the cost for plastic-wrapped sprigs from the supermarket. From live poultry to tableware, you'll find everything you need to prepare an authentic Asian meal. The nearby shops sell Vietnamese-style pâtés and deli meats, baked goods, and imported groceries.

The market begins around dawn, and that is the best time to go, when you will find the best choice of goods. Vendors start drifting away an hour or two before the market offi-cially ends at 10 A.M. Dark French-drip coffee, along with a stand-up breakfast of spicy pork po-boys or steamed buns, will help get your eyes open. The atmosphere is chaotic but friendly, a hubbub of bargaining, gossip, and loud Vietnamese pop music.

Martin Wine Cellar

Another great source for exotic culinary imports, Martin Wine Cellar has become a renowned general store for gourmet foods. When David Martin first began doing business in 1946, his shop sold mainly cigarettes and soda. To save money he would unscrew the lightbulbs until a potential customer came into sight. Every penny he pinched was invested in extra inventory, which has since grown to include thousands of wines and hundreds of beers and cheeses, as well as fresh smoked salmon, pâtés, caviars, and New York–style deli meats. Along with the original Uptown location, there is a second branch located in suburban Metairie.

Because liquor prices in Louisiana are low, many regular customers come from as far as Mississippi, Alabama, and Texas to stock up. The store is also supported by locals, as well as tourists and conventioneers, and a thriving mail-order business serves out-of-state clients from coast to coast, with overseas shipments routed as far away as Switzerland.

FLAVORS OF THE NEIGHBORHOODS

In its earliest days, the French Quarter *was* New Orleans, and it still is for many visitors who choose to stay within those one hundred square blocks. But this gorgeous city has plenty of other neighborhoods worth exploring, and delicious adventures await travelers who venture beyond Bourbon Street.

French Quarter

Here are the gaslights and tropical courtyards of the tourist brochures, the promise of grand dining at Antoine's, Brennan's, Broussard's, Galatoire's, Tujague's, and other historic landmarks. You can also get a taste of Creole classics (and a smaller check) at The Gumbo Shop and The Old Coffee Pot, or linger for hours at atmospheric Napoleon House and Crescent City Brewhouse. Café du Monde has been open around the clock since the 1860s, an essential destination for beignets, café au lait, and people watching. Stop in for serious Cajun cooking at K-Paul's Louisiana Kitchen —home base of star chef Paul Prudhomme— or try Susan Spicer's celebrated New World cuisine at Bayona. Contemporary Creole is on the menu at The Bistro at Maison de Ville, Nola, Peristyle, Pelican Club, G&E Courtyard Grill, and Mr. B's Bistro.

Central Grocery has been a local favorite since 1906, a crowded and colorful Sicilian deli that wraps its famous muffulettas to go (for a picnic on the riverfront Moonwalk). Bella Luna and Irene's Cuisine are best for a romantic Italian dinner. The Louisiana General Store peddles regional kitchen supplies and half-day cooking classes. Posh and pricey Lucullus stocks museum-quality cooking and dining pieces, such as rare and sumptuous French china, stemware, and flatware from the seventeenth through the twentieth century.

Despite the antiquated atmosphere and the hustle of tourism, the French Quarter remains a vibrant neighborhood, where locals continue to live, work, and play. Residents still attend Mass at stately St. Louis Cathedral. They purchase fresh produce at the outdoor French Market and stock their kitchens at the A&P Supermarket on Royal Street, a busy old neighborhood corner grocery where visitors can fill their carts with culinary souvenirs at hometown prices, shopping alongside off-duty musicians, bartenders, and fortune tellers.

Faubourg Marigny

Bernard Marigny had gambled away most of his fortune by 1808, so he subdivided the family plantation into lots, creating this early faubourg (suburb) that now borders the French Quarter in the center of town. The dividing line is drawn by Esplanade Avenue, an oak-draped boulevard graced by mansions that recall the glory days of the nineteenth century, when New Orleans was a wealthy commercial and shipping center second only to New York.

Like its namesake, Faubourg Marigny is wayward and careless, home to Bohemians and artists driven out of the French Quarter by skyrocketing rents and creeping tourism. Culinary stars of the neighborhood are the critically acclaimed Café Marigny, with its seasonal eclectic menu, and Feelings Café d'Aunoy. You'll also find Snug Harbor, a cool

haven for enjoying char-grilled burgers while listening to the modern masters of sound. Adventurers can table hop around the world, enjoying late-night sounds and snacks at Café Brasil, Café Siam, and other hangouts of the nouveau-tattooed.

Central Business District (CBD)

Office buildings and convention hotels dominate the economic heart of the city, where you'll find big-name shops and options for casual dining at a trio of shopping centers, Canal Place, New Orleans Centre, and the waterfront Riverwalk Marketplace. Grand cuisine and formal service reign in the Grill Room at Windsor Court and Victor's at the Ritz-Carlton. The Bon Ton Cafe is the city's oldest Cajun-style restaurant, a business lunch destination for more than fifty years. Hearty Southern breakfasts and generous po-boys have earned a national reputation for Mother's. Other local favorites include Palace Café, Uglesich's, Liborio's Cuban Restaurant, and The Pearl.

Warehouse-Arts District

Some of the city's best galleries have taken over the historic warehouses and lofts that were once occupied by cotton presses and ship chandlers in "the SoHo of the South," surrounded by several downtown blocks of elegant nineteenth-century buildings with original cast-iron work and Gothic arches. Culinary arts are on display at Zöe Bistrot, Emeril's, Herbsaint, and Gerard's Downtown. Theater and other entertainments are presented at the massive Contemporary Arts Center and also at True Brew Coffee and Le Chat Noir.

Garden District and Uptown

The St. Charles Avenue streetcar clangs past the nineteenth-century mansions of the Garden District, continuing into the adjoining neighborhood known simply as Uptown, home to Tulane and Loyola universities and many of the city's social elite. Running parallel to St. Charles Avenue, but several blocks closer to the river, is fun and funky Magazine Street,

an ever-evolving jumble of markets, bistros, ethnic cafés, antiques dealers, contemporary art galleries, vintage clothing and furniture shops, crafters, New Age practitioners, and taverns. Both streets follow the curve of the Mississippi to the cozy old enclave of Riverbend, with its upscale restaurants, boutiques, and artisans' studios.

Commander's Palace anchors the culinary scene, rambling throughout a turreted Victorian with a courtyard garden, across the street from the historic tombs of Lafayette Cemetery. Stylish Louisiana cuisine also shines in the warm and colorful dining rooms of The Upperline, a bright yellow townhouse filled with folk art and flowers. Well-heeled Uptowners also like the dapper atmosphere at Gautreau's and Clancy's, as well as the downhome fare at Jacques-Imo's. Unlike other nationally acclaimed chef-proprietors, Frank Brigtsen still mans the stove nearly every night at Brigtsen's. Dick and Jenny's is also supported by loyal local followers who love the contemporary Creole cuisine and

youthful attitude. Camellia Grill is a stately old white-columned diner positioned under the oak trees where breakfast queues stretch down the sidewalk on weekends. Near the universities, quaint little Maple Street is lined with cottages housing bookstores, ethnic cafés, coffeehouses, and bars that attract the young and the restless.

Mid-City

The vast urban neighborhood known as Mid-City incorporates the Bayou St. John Historic District, a languid waterfront neighborhood of antebellum plantation houses and Victorian cottages, and the deep green shade of Esplanade Avenue and City Park, a fifteen-hundred-acre (six-hundred-hectare) oasis of moss-draped oaks and gardens, home to the New Orleans Museum of Art. Fine dining awaits at the charming and contemporary Gabrielle, Christian's (set in a former church), Ralph's on the Park, and the original Ruth's Chris Steak House. Famed chef Leah Chase presides over a stellar combination of Creole soul food and regional folk art at Dooky Chase, an urban landmark since 1941.

Smart and youthful Mid-City dwellers love the Parisian-style Café Degas, paella at Lola's, fragrant Vietnamese soups at Pho Tau Bay, Lebanese feasts at Mona's, and Sicilian sweets at Angelo Brocato's Ice Cream and Confectionery. Mid-City Lanes is the vintage 1940s setting for Rock 'n' Bowl, a wild and noisy conglomeration of Cajun and Creole food, live music, and bowling.

Lakefront

In the early twentieth century, lawmen turned a blind eye to gambling and other vices at lakefront honky-tonks and speakeasies, where Buddy Bolden and Louis Armstrong once played at parties that raged for days. During the 1940s and 1950s, barrooms rang with illegal pinballs and slot machines. Today the scene is much calmer and family oriented.

But if the vice is largely gone, the lake views still go on forever at casual seafood restaurants such as Bruning's and Jaeger's. The Southern Yacht Club overlooks a busy marina filled with pleasure boats. Independent fishermen moor their small craft in the nearby commercial harbor, supplying the fresh catch for seafood markets and restaurants in Bucktown, where the hungry masses head to comfortable old Sid-Mar's, Deanie's, and R&O for platters of fresh seafood and po-boys stuffed with fried oysters. Locals love the traditional Italian food at upscale Tony Angello's, a real treat for indecisive diners who can order a multicourse tasting dinner that changes daily.

Metairie

Meaning "small farms" in French, Metairie refers to a once-agricultural area that is now a metropolitan bedroom community at the western edge of New Orleans. Genteel Old Metairie, a residential area centered around Metairie Road, is a stronghold of wealthy families and young professionals who go for upscale ethnic fare at Vega Tapas Cafe, Taj Mahal, La Thai Cuisine, and the French-accented DeVille Bistro. The newer suburban area known simply as Metairie is littered with chain restaurants, but it also offers classic Italian dining at Andrea's and Ristorante La Riviera, as well as seafood at Bozo's (a favorite for more than seventy-five years) and Drago's, famed for its char-grilled oysters.

The West Bank

In addition to a gorgeous ride aboard the Canal Street ferry across the bustling port of New Orleans, the best reason for foodies to visit the suburban and industrial area that lies on the other side of the Mississippi River is the collection of eateries that serve its huge Vietnamese community. Among the best are the original Pho Tau Bay Restaurant (and the adjoining Kim Phat Oriental Food Market), Nine Roses, and Kim Son.

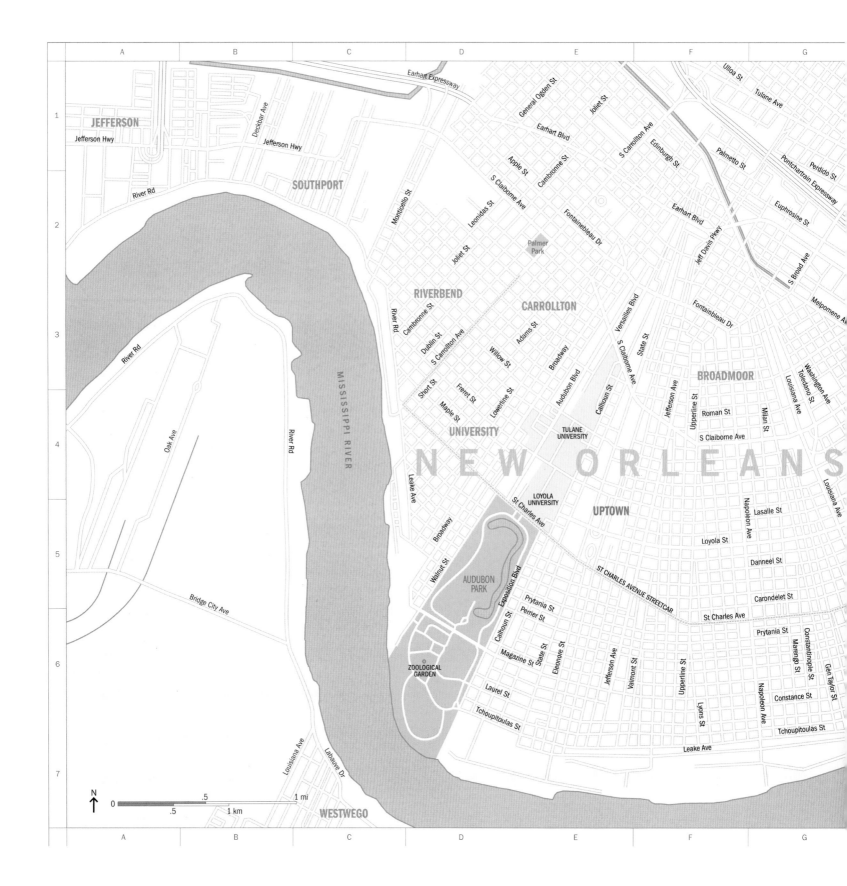

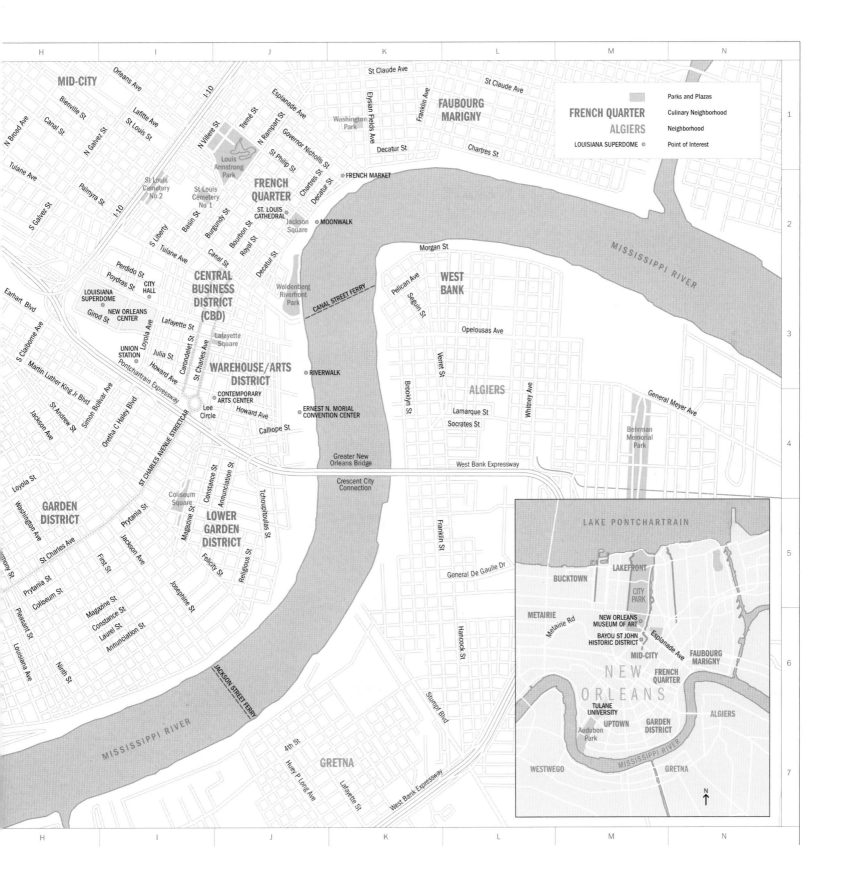

MID-CITY

Orleans Ave
Bienville St
Lafitte Ave
St Louis St
N Broad Ave
Canal St
N Galvez St
Tulane Ave
Palmyra St
S Galvez St

St Louis
Cemetery
No 2

St Louis
Cemetery
No 1

Louis
Armstrong
Park

I-10

N Villere St
Tremé St
N Rampart St
Governor Nicholls St
St Philip St
Burgundy St
Bourbon St
Royal St

Esplanade Ave

FRENCH
QUARTER

ST. LOUIS
CATHEDRAL

Jackson
Square

● MOONWALK

Chartres St
Decatur St

● FRENCH MARKET

St Claude Ave

St Claude Ave

Elysian Fields Ave

Washington
Park

Franklin Ave

FAUBOURG
MARIGNY

Decatur St
Chartres St

FRENCH QUARTER
ALGIERS
● LOUISIANA SUPERDOME

Parks and Plazas
Culinary Neighborhood
Neighborhood
Point of Interest

MISSISSIPPI RIVER

Basin St
S Liberty
S Tulane Ave
Canal St
Decatur St

Earhart Blvd
S Claiborne Ave

Perdido St
Poydras St
CITY
HALL

LOUISIANA
SUPERDOME

NEW ORLEANS
CENTER

Girod St

CENTRAL
BUSINESS
DISTRICT
(CBD)

Woldenberg
Riverfront
Park

CANAL STREET FERRY

Morgan St

Pelican Ave
Seguin St

WEST
BANK

Opelousas Ave

Loyola Ave
Lafayette St
Carondelet St
St Charles Ave
Union Station
Julia St
Howard Ave

Lafayette
Square

WAREHOUSE/ARTS
DISTRICT

CONTEMPORARY
ARTS CENTER

Lee
Circle

Howard Ave

Calliope St

● RIVERWALK

ERNEST N. MORIAL
CONVENTION CENTER

Verret St

Brooklyn St

ALGIERS

Lamarque St
Socrates St

Whitney Ave

General Meyer Ave

Behrman
Memorial
Park

Pontchartrain Expressway

Martin Luther King Jr Blvd
Simon Bolivar Ave
Oretha C Haley Blvd

Jackson Ave
St Andrew St

Loyola St

Washington Ave

St Charles Ave

Pleasant St
Louisiana Ave
Ninth St
Josephine St
Religious St
Felicity St

GARDEN
DISTRICT

Coliseum
Square

Prytania St
Jackson Ave

Constance St
Annunciation St

LOWER
GARDEN
DISTRICT

Magazine St

Tchoupitoulas St

Greater New
Orleans Bridge

Crescent City
Connection

West Bank Expressway

Franklin St

General De Gaulle Dr

Hancock St

Stumpf Blvd

Prytania St
First St
Coliseum St
Magazine St
Constance St
Laurel St
Annunciation St

JACKSON STREET FERRY

MISSISSIPPI RIVER

4th St
Huey P Long Ave

GRETNA

Lafayette St

West Bank Expressway

LAKE PONTCHARTRAIN

BUCKTOWN

LAKEFRONT

CITY
PARK

METAIRIE

Metairie Rd

NEW ORLEANS
MUSEUM OF ART

BAYOU ST JOHN
HISTORIC DISTRICT

Esplanade Ave

MID-CITY

FAUBOURG
MARIGNY

NEW

ORLEANS

FRENCH
QUARTER

TULANE
UNIVERSITY

UPTOWN

GARDEN
DISTRICT

ALGIERS

Audubon
Park

WESTWEGO

MISSISSIPPI RIVER

GRETNA

N

Best of **NEW ORLEANS**

The excesses of Bourbon Street and Mardi Gras are well known, and indeed, this is a city where bars outnumber churches and remain open around the clock. Here, travelers can still enjoy a dignified drink at truly historic meeting spots, worn smooth by generations of good times and easygoing company.

BARS AND COCKTAILS

When it comes to colorful history, no bar can beat Napoleon House, built in 1797 by a former mayor of New Orleans. It was once prepared as a home for the exiled emperor by local Bonapartists in an elaborate plot to rescue him from the island of St. Helena (his death in 1821 thwarted their plans). Dark and intimate, with a cozy little courtyard, it has been a favored watering hole since 1914, and is still an oasis of classical recordings, witty conversation, and French colonial atmosphere.

Lafitte's Blacksmith Shop (built circa 1722) leans a bit, but it has weathered floods, fires, and hurricanes to survive as the city's second-oldest building (after the Old Ursuline Convent). A fine example of early post-and-brick construction, it now houses a popular piano bar—a welcome retreat from the clatter of nearby Bourbon Street.

The long-standing bar adjoining Tujague's Restaurant on Decatur Street is a polished cypress beauty, still backed by the ornately framed mirror shipped from Paris to celebrate the establishment's debut in 1856. Service wasn't interrupted even during Prohibition, when liquor was poured into coffee cups and the supply was hidden in an air shaft.

Uptown, when you cross the enormous veranda and enter the Columns Hotel on St. Charles Avenue, you'll feel like you've walked onto the set of *Pretty Baby*—and you have. The faded grandeur of the 1883 mansion was perfect for Louis Malle's film about a Jazz Age bordello. The lobby's Victorian Lounge is a comfy pub plumped with velvet upholstery, carved woodwork, and pressed tin.

The power drinking crowd favors the Sazerac Bar in the lobby of the Central Business District's Fairmont Hotel, a clubby sanctuary of walnut paneling and tile floors. Largely unchanged since the 1930s, it is dominated by Paul Ninas's vintage murals of the French Market and other local scenes.

Famous for its rum Hurricanes, crowded and lively Pat O'Brien's in the French Quarter is tourist central, with a huge courtyard and pianists who pound out college fight songs. Established in 1933, it has been a landmark at its St. Peter Street location since 1942.

The revolving Carousel Bar has been in operation since the 1940s, when it was installed in the lobby of the Monteleone Hotel in the French Quarter. Grand and gilded, like an enormous antique merry-go-round, it glides past large windows overlooking Royal Street. Truman Capote and Tennessee Williams were among its regulars.

In New Orleans, self-indulgence is a birthright and drinking is a civilized pursuit.

Today, drinks at the Old Absinthe House are made with Herbsaint—a legal version of absinthe, minus the narcotic kick of wormwood—and the crumbling Bourbon Street bar is cluttered with football memorabilia and thousands of business cards stapled on the walls. Even so, you'll still see traces of the belle epoque, when the "green fairy" was in residence.

Old Absinthe House

A portrait of the Old Absinthe House is engraved on the label of the Herbsaint bottle, while on the back is the (updated) recipe for the drink that made it famous. Among the countless notables who bellied up to the bar for the celebrated absinthe frappé were Mark Twain, Oscar Wilde, and William Thackeray. Preserved along the cypress bar are marble fountains that once dripped cool water over sugar cubes into glasses filled with cloudy swirls of pale green absinthe.

Herbsaint History

Ever since absinthe—the notorious "green fairy"—was declared a bit too magical for human consumption, distillers worldwide have concocted anise-flavored potions without wormwood, a psychoactive herb outlawed in 1912. Today's kindred spirits are known as pastis in France, ouzo in Greece, *anis* in Spain, and raki in Turkey. North America's only *liqueur d'anis* is produced in New Orleans by the Sazerac Company, and even though its wings have been clipped, ninety-proof Herbsaint still spins a powerful spell.

In the nineteenth and early twentieth centuries, several Louisiana brands of absinthe were available. All contained wormwood, a fragrant, gray-green plant that was called *herbe sainte* by the French-speaking population. Today, old labels like Green Opal and Milky Way have vanished in a green mist. Only Herbsaint remains.

The chartreuse hue and complex flavor of Herbsaint may be startling in a glass, but the flowery licorice taste is a natural in the kitchen. It's essential for dishes like oysters Rockefeller and for many classic New Orleans cocktails.

Making a Sazerac

COATING THE GLASS The Sazerac is the signature cocktail of high society in New Orleans, originally made with Sazerac de Forge brandy, hence the name. The version we know today was created in the late nineteenth century by Leon Lamothe, who replaced the brandy with rye whiskey. Instead of the absinthe that was formerly used (since outlawed in the United States), most bartenders now use Herbsaint. To begin, drizzle a small amount of Herbsaint into an old-fashioned glass, swirl to coat the inside, and pour off any excess.

SHAKING THE COCKTAIL Pour the rye whiskey into a cocktail shaker. Add simple syrup, along with several dashes of Angostura bitters or Peychaud bitters (produced locally by the Sazerac Company and named for the pharmacist who invented the cocktail). Shake the mixture with ice cubes until it is well chilled.

SERVING THE COCKTAIL Strain the mixture into the prepared old-fashioned glass and garnish with a twist of lemon peel.

MINT JULEP

PIMM'S CUP

CAJUN MARTINI

BRANDY MILK PUNCH

MINT JULEP

Originating in Persia, where the word *julâb* means "rose water," sweet syrup mixed with liquor or medication has been known as a julep in England since the fifteenth century. British colonials brought the beverage to the Caribbean and North America, where it evolved into the official drink of Dixie, a symbol of Southern hospitality from the Louisiana cane fields to the Kentucky Derby. Fresh mint leaves are muddled with bourbon and sugar syrup in a tall glass or silver mug, which is then packed to the rim with crushed ice. Cliché, yes—but a comfort indeed on a humid summer day.

PIMM'S CUP

Ironic that a British drink should be the specialty at Napoleon House, once a hotbed of Bonapartist conspiracy, but New Orleanians have always been a pragmatic people, especially when they're hot and thirsty. Pimm's Cup is a fine remedy, further cooled by its distinctive garnish, a slice of fresh cucumber. Basically a well-iced highball in a Tom Collins glass, it's made with England's gin-based liqueur, Pimm's No. 1, topped off with ginger ale or club soda. Some people like to add lemon or lime juice, plus the extra flourish of a mint sprig.

CAJUN MARTINI

Martinis have been hot stuff since Martini & Rossi vermouth first met gin, but the Louisiana spin-off is more recent, a product of the Cajun cooking craze led by chef Paul Prudhomme in the 1980s. Suddenly America developed a taste for fire—and plenty of it—and everything wild and spicy was labeled "Cajun," including a strictly nontraditional cocktail made with pepper vodka. It's generally garnished with a jalapeño-stuffed olive or a pod of hot pickled okra—a fun novelty for a backyard cookout or seafood boil, but not likely to tempt James Bond.

BRANDY MILK PUNCH

During the holidays, when residents of colder climates brew mulled wine or hot buttered rum, New Orleanians are more likely to offer guests an icy cup of this old-fashioned indulgence. Although bourbon or rum is some-times used, the drink is more commonly made with brandy, sweetened with superfine (caster) sugar, and whipped to a froth with milk or cream, then topped by a sprinkle of grated nutmeg. Brandy milk punch is also a traditional eye-opener served with weekend brunch, and at the famous Breakfast at Brennan's, where a full punch bowl is always kept on ice at the bar.

HURRICANE

HERBSAINT
FRAPPÉ

RAMOS GIN
FIZZ

SAZERAC

HURRICANE

Everybody has to try it at least once. The quintessential tourist drink is a potent cure for those hometown inhibitions, a whirlwind of sweet punch and a hearty measure of rum, appropriately served in a glass shaped like a hurricane lamp. Retro and quirky, it has been the house specialty at Pat O'Brien's since World War II, when local liquor distributors were running low on everything but rum, and an enter-prising salesman helped the bar develop the now-famous drink, spiked with tropical fruit flavors and garnished with an orange slice and a maraschino cherry.

SAZERAC

Hailed as the "royal libation of Rex, king of Mardi Gras," the Sazerac is believed by some to be the world's first cocktail. According to legend, it was created in the 1830s by apothecary Antoine Peychaud, who entertained friends after hours at his pharmacy with a mix of absinthe, brandy, and bitters served in egg cups, or *coquetiers,* later anglicized to "cocktails." Around 1890 the original Sazerac Bar popularized the version still served today, made with rye whiskey (instead of brandy), Peychaud's Bitters, sugar syrup, and a lemon twist. Herbsaint has since replaced the outlawed absinthe.

HERBSAINT FRAPPÉ

Like other anise liqueurs, Herbsaint turns cloudy when water is added. For the French-style frappé, ice water is dripped over a sugar lump set atop a pierced spoon that is balanced across a glass of Herbsaint, sweetening the bitter liqueur and slowly causing it to swirl into wispy clouds. Patiently executed, the visual effect can be magical. As described in a rather lurid passage in a 1944 recipe booklet distributed by the Sazerac Company, the process transforms the clear chartreuse Herbsaint into "an opaque beverage whose gyrating whorls of coalescent strata have a distinct opalescent hue."

RAMOS GIN FIZZ

The ethereal texture of this refreshing cooler comes from whipped egg whites, the fizz from club soda, the delicate flavor from orange flower water. One of the great signature drinks of New Orleans, it was concocted by bar owner Henry Ramos in the 1880s. Today it is whirred in a blender and enriched by light (single) cream, confectioners' (icing) sugar, lemon or lime juice, and vanilla. A luxurious prelude to a Creole brunch, it was a favorite of Louisiana's Depression-era governor Huey Long, the legendary Kingfish.

One thing is aways certain: Somewhere in Louisiana there will be dancing in the streets this weekend, whether it is a music festival or an obscure saint's day. You can count on real food—not just cotton candy and funnel cakes—at all regional festivities, because it takes plenty of fuel to keep those good times rolling.

FESTIVALS AND HOLIDAYS

The biggest party of the year is the New Orleans Jazz and Heritage Festival in late April and early May, a massive blowout that has become an even bigger draw than Mardi Gras. Music and food share center stage, with vendors offering indigenous eats, from fried alligator to pheasant gumbo, along with more recent additions to the local melting pot, such as Vietnamese spring rolls, Tunisian lamb sausage, and Cuban tamales. Competition is fierce to snag one of the seventy-five food booths, and all must present traditional dishes from one of the ethnic groups that populate the city. In recent years, many music fans have been drawn west of the Crescent City by the concurrent Festival International de Louisiane in Lafayette, the hub of Cajun country, where regional food and music are more narrowly defined.

Harvest celebrations fill the state calendar with dozens of festivals devoted to such delicacies as Creole tomatoes, strawberries, peaches, watermelon, pecans, rice, catfish, crawfish, oysters, crabs, rabbits, frogs, and suckling pigs. Each October the Louisiana Yambilee glorifies the sweet potato in the town of Opelousas, Zydeco Capital of the World and hometown to Cajun superchef Paul Prudhomme. Also in October, the St. Martinville Pepper Festival on Bayou Teche is a simple pleasure for hotheads, offering spicy Cajun fare and locally brewed sauces. When November blows into Basile, young ladies compete for the dubious honor of being queen of the Louisiana Swine Festival.

A gala blessing of the shrimp fleet (see page 111) is usually scheduled in July or August at fishing communities in Delcambre,

Grand Isle, Yscloskey, Jean Lafitte, and Delacroix. The oddly named Shrimp and Petroleum Festival in Morgan City recognizes workers from both the seafood and oil industries and includes the blessing of a procession of shrimpers, Sunday fishers, and huge "muscle boats" from the oil patch.

Good cooks get fired up at various fests devoted to jambalaya, andouille, cracklins, Cajun food, or chili. Regardless of the name, most events will feature at least one type of gumbo, but none can approach the variety of the World Championship Gumbo Cookoff each October in New Iberia, where more than fifty competing teams stock their pots with the usual chicken and seafood, but also rabbits, quail, alligators, ducks, and other exotica.

However, the single most impressive dish is created every November at the Giant

Holidays, music, and food—any reason is a good reason for a festival.

Omelette Celebration in Abbeville, a tradition shared with its sister city, Bessières, France. Following an Omelette Mass at the Catholic church, dignitaries and chefs lead the Procession of the Eggs, carrying some five thousand that will be cooked in a giant frying pan, lowered by forklift over a bonfire, and stirred with equally giant paddles.

New Orleanians observe Epiphany with the first of many king cakes (page 170) that will disrupt classrooms and workplaces for weeks to come. It's the official kickoff of Carnival—from the Latin *carnem levare,* meaning roughly "farewell to meat"—a season of generalized overindulgence that crashes on Ash Wednesday, which begins forty days of

the poor bird through the mud, over fences, and under buildings, to the cheers of a crowd of onlookers.

To honor St. Patrick on March 17, Irish bars in New Orleans dispense green beer, while marching groups toss whole cabbages to spectators. Italian American parades commemorate the Feast Day of St. Joseph on March 19, along with a unique custom that dates back to the Middle Ages. When medieval Sicilians petitioned their patron to deliver them from a famine, and rains saved the fava (broad) bean crop, they erected a food-laden altar in gratitude. Their New Orleans descendants carry on the tradition, creating fantastic St. Joseph altars in

The same day they dismantle their Christmas trees, New Orleanians jump right into Carnival, weeks of parades and balls beginning January 6—just one of 365 reasons to celebrate in a town where the calendar revolves around food and drink.

fasting and atonement for Lent. It is preceded by the frenzied final bender known as Mardi Gras, French for "Fat Tuesday," when the *boeuf gras* (a fiberglass version of Europe's traditional fatted calf) is paraded through New Orleans, launching a citywide street party with plenty of other flesh on display.

Meanwhile, out in Cajun country, it's a bad day for chickens. The Carnival rite of masked men galloping from house to house collecting ingredients for a community gumbo, a holdover from similar European rituals that date back to the Middle Ages, has survived for centuries in southwestern Louisiana. During the Courir du Mardi Gras (Fat Tuesday Run), riders thunder into farmyards to sing, dance atop their saddles, and *faites des macaques* (make monkeyshines) for the customary reward of a *poule grasse* (fat chicken). The maskers must catch it themselves, chasing

churches and homes. Each visitor is given a lucky dried fava bean to keep in his or her wallet (so it will never be empty).

Halloween is always spectacular in this spooky old city that loves masquerades, ghosts, and unhealthy treats. On the following All Saints' Day, the faithful visit cemeteries to clean family tombs, a semisomber occasion that sometimes incorporates picnics or toasts to the departed.

Holiday events throughout December include wine tastings, restaurant specials, and plantations decked with lights. On Christmas Eve more than one hundred bonfires line Mississippi levees upriver from New Orleans, a tradition since the nineteenth century, to guide Papa Noël as he paddles his pirogue (a Cajun-style canoe) to deliver gifts to Louisiana children. New Year's Day brings black-eyed peas (for luck) and cabbage (for money).

Far from abandoning its farmyard roots in this age of low-fat dining and growing vegetarianism, Louisiana celebrates its favorite meat, from festive roasts of suckling pig, or *cochon de lait,* on warm spring afternoons to the community hog butchering known as *la boucherie* in the chilly days of winter.

CHARCUTERIE

"Everything but the oink" is the motto on the prairies of south Louisiana, where Cajuns descended from frugal Gallic farmers make use of the whole animal, wasting as little as possible. They preserve the old ways of charcuterie (from the French *cuiseur de chair,* meaning "cooker of meat"), stocking their larders with home-cured hams, smoked sausages, and pickled pork.

The port city of New Orleans was settled largely by the French, along with other immigrant populations who imported traditions of their own. The colonnaded market across from Jackson Square (now Café du Monde and a string of souvenir shops) once housed the massive Halle des Boucheries, a nineteenth-century congregation of German butchers. The nearby Central Grocery helped popularize Sicilian-style deli meats, which are

essential for the local muffuletta sandwiches (page 135), while sweet Italian sausages are stuffed into po-boys or simmered with Creole white beans and rice. Recent arrivals include French-Vietnamese pâtés and sausages.

Most large Louisiana groceries still produce their own fresh sausages and charcuterie. Among the best grocers are locally owned and operated Langenstein's in New Orleans, Dorignac's in suburban Metairie, and the regional Rouse's Supermarkets chain. Worth a special drive, slow-smoked sausages and meats are outstanding at Taaffe's Hogshead Cheese and Sausage in Chalmette and Wayne Jacob's Smokehouse in LaPlace.

Influential chefs such as Paul Prudhomme and Emeril Lagasse have reintroduced classic charcuterie to the restaurant kitchens of New Orleans, improving the quality of the meats that

are served to their guests, while encouraging the young culinarians who work in their kitchens to learn skills that support regional growers and keep the old ways alive. Those vanishing crafts are also preserved at regional festivals, such as La Grande Boucherie at St. Martinville in February, the massive Cochon de Lait Festival at Mansura each May, and the November Cracklin Festival in Port Barre.

Fear not, health enthusiasts. In recent years, leaner (although not exactly fat-free) turkey has often been substituted for pork in traditional charcuterie. Many regional markets now stock smoked turkey legs (to season the bean pot in place of ham hocks), as well as turkey andouille, tasso, Italian sausages, boudin, and even hogshead cheese, which is usually stuck with the equally unappetizing label "turkey head cheese."

Slow-pot cooking in Louisiana calls for smokehouse hams and sausages.

MUFFULETTA

CONSISTS OF

Imported Salami, Ham & Cheese,
Mortadella
"Our Special Olive Salad"
on Italian Bread

ANDOUILLE

BOUDIN

HAM

TASSO

ANDOUILLE

To create the king of Louisiana sausages, a long casing is stuffed with lean chunks of ham, highly seasoned with salt and pepper, and slow-smoked into a dense and wrinkly link that could be the size of a wiener or a rolling pin, depending on its maker. Andouille (pronounced on-DOO-ee) is the premier ingredient in gumbos and jambalayas and a traditional accompaniment for red beans. It is also very tasty grilled with a sweet-hot dip of pepper jelly (page 158), or cradled in French bread and topped with creamy red beans for a Cajun hot dog.

BOUDIN

For white boudin (pronounced BOO-dan), minced green (spring) onions, rice, and other seasonings are stuffed into casings with finely ground pork. Well-spiced and appealingly tender, it's the pride of Cajun country, prepared with great care at gas stations, convenience stores, and small-town groceries. Wrapped in butcher paper and presented with a pack of saltines, it's best consumed hot in the parking lot. Free maps of the Boudin Trail are available at tourist information centers. Black or red boudin is a blood sausage prepared mainly by home cooks.

HAM

In Louisiana, as in the rest of the South, a baked ham is the symbol of abundance and hospitality. A roasted fresh ham is an interesting alternative, with a flavor more similar to pork roast and a drier and denser texture produced by curing the meat overnight in a Cajun-style rub of coarse salt, pepper, and other spices. After Sunday dinner, chunks of ham are sure to appear in everything from scrambled eggs to smothered cabbage. And no Louisiana cook would dream of wasting the bone, when it lends such smoky depth to a pot of beans or split pea soup.

TASSO

The lean Cajun-style ham known as tasso (pronounced TOSS-oh) is very dry and dense, smoke-cured in savory little chunks that are rubbed with plenty of salt, pepper, filé (ground sassafras leaves), and other spices. Because of its tough and leathery consistency, which tenderizes into chewy shreds when stewed, it is used primarily as a flavoring for slow-pot foods, such as beans and gumbo. It is also a fine addition to jambalaya, re-creating the taste and texture of the air-cured Spanish-style ham that was probably used in the original version.

PICKLED PORK

CRACKLINS

FRESH SAUSAGES

HOGSHEAD CHEESE

PICKLED PORK

Also known as pickle meat, pieces of fresh pork, such as shoulder, are cured for several days in vinegar seasoned with salt, garlic, mustard seeds, peppercorns, bay leaves, and allspice. Reminiscent of corned beef in both color and flavor, the tangy pickled pork is traditionally used to flavor red beans and other vegetables. In the spirit of "everything but the oink," various other cuts of pork are preserved in a similar brew and presented in large jars at country barrooms, where patrons who are so inclined may snack on pickled pig's feet, lips, or snouts.

CRACKLINS

Fried pork rinds have achieved an unlikely popularity in recent years, mainly because they add desired crunch to low-carb diets, but the authentic version is a world away from the Styrofoam-like snack you'll find sold in plastic bags. Real cracklins, known in French Louisiana as *gratons,* are made by slowly frying strips of pork skin in a kettle of boiling oil (preferably rendered pork fat) until they curl into tasty little crisps, which are then seasoned with salt and at least two kinds of pepper. They're also good crumbled into batter for cracklin corn bread.

FRESH SAUSAGES

Ground pork sausage seasons Cajun rice dressings, stuffed bell peppers (capsicums), and meat loaf. Common varieties include an anise-scented Italian sausage, a savory sausage flecked with chopped green (spring) onions, and the brick red "hot sausage" supercharged with cayenne. Packed into casings, they add substance to a pot of beans or soak up the highly spiced water at a seafood boil. Simmered in a rich red gravy, a single link joins a large meatball atop a mound of pasta for the local Sicilian special known as "spaghetti with a ball and bat."

HOGSHEAD CHEESE

Talk about a marketing liability! Hogshead cheese is an ugly name for what is essentially chopped pork in a stiff and spicy aspic seasoned with cayenne pepper, green (spring) onions, and other seasonings. In bygone days it was made with hog jowls, hence the name, but now it is more likely to contain shreds from the meaty shoulder, or butt, roast. It is often chilled in small loaf pans, so each slice will fit comfortably on a saltine. Like much of Louisiana charcuterie, it definitely tastes better than it sounds.

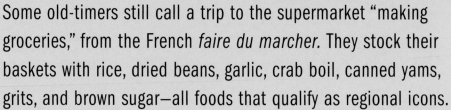

Some old-timers still call a trip to the supermarket "making groceries," from the French *faire du marcher.* They stock their baskets with rice, dried beans, garlic, crab boil, canned yams, grits, and brown sugar—all foods that qualify as regional icons.

FOOD ICONS

What's on most tables in south Louisiana, besides the salt and pepper? Count on at least two brands of hot sauce and maybe more, since everyone has his or her own preference. Hundreds of spicy brews are bottled, and dozens are commonly available, including the ubiquitous Tabasco, Crystal Hot Sauce, and Trappey's Red Devil.

Kept handy near many stoves, cylindrical boxes of Cajun or Creole seasoning typically shake out a blend of cayenne pepper, salt, paprika, garlic powder, and assorted spices. Among the most popular brands are Tony Chachere's, Zatarain's, and Konriko.

Filé (pronounced FEE-lay), used as a thickener and flavoring in some gumbos, was contributed to the culinary melting pot by native Choctaws. The khaki green powder is ground from sassafras leaves.

Some French Quarter visitors will go home with hangovers, but nobody can keep up the pace of hard-drinking tourists in daily life. Actually, the unofficial "house wine of the South" is iced tea. In Louisiana that usually means Luzianne or Community, also two of the most popular local brands for coffee, along with Café du Monde (CDM). In recent years, relative newcomer PJ's Coffee & Tea Company has captured a big share of the upscale market.

New Orleans still claims its own soft drink brands as well, although both have been acquired by national corporations. Barq's Root Beer, established in 1898, remains the city's signature soda. The original company also created vanilla-flavored Barq's Red Crème Soda, for generations known simply as "red drink." Less common but equally fun is the vintage Big Shot Pineapple Soda, with its cigar-chomping ward boss on the label.

Creole cream cheese is a soft disk of fresh farmer's cheese (similar to Neufchâtel), traditionally afloat in a pint container filled to the brim with heavy cream. It's a lavish treat for breakfast (with sugar and fresh berries) or churned into a tangy ice cream. Once produced by several local dairies, now it's not easy to find, although you can still buy it at Dorignac's market in suburban Metairie, or Mauthe's Dairy at the Crescent City Farmers' Market.

An old-fashioned breakfast in Louisiana goes way beyond ham and eggs, cushioning the morning landing with hot buttermilk biscuits, pecan waffles, or sweet potato muffins, made from such soft-wheat Southern flours as White Lily or Martha White, which are lower in stretchy gluten.

These essential products add color to Louisiana kitchens and classic dishes.

DIXIE BEER   ZATARAIN'S CREOLE   PICKLED OKRA   TABASCO   HUBIG'S PIES

MUSTARD

DIXIE BEER

The last of the old-time New Orleans beers is still produced at the Dixie Brewing Company on Tulane Avenue in Mid-City, where it has been bottled since 1907. Aged in cypress barrels, the original lager is light and dry, a refreshing thirst quencher that's just right with spicy boiled seafood or a tray of briny iced oysters on the half shell. Competition from upstart microbrews, such as the very popular Abita beer, has inspired recent additions to the line, including Dixie Blackened Voodoo Lager, a kitschy name for a dark and slightly tart *schwarzbier*.

ZATARAIN'S CREOLE MUSTARD

Hotter than German-style brown mustard, creamier than French-style whole-grain *moutarde,* Creole mustard is smooth and zesty, assertive enough for the flavor to sparkle through the mayonnaise and gravy on a roast beef po-boy. One of the original products created by Zatarain's founder Emile Zatarain, it has been bottled in New Orleans since 1889. Dense with flecks of stone-ground mustard seeds, it resides in refrigerator doors through-out Louisiana, where cooks stir it into potato salads, vinaigrettes, baked beans, barbecue sauces, and sweet glazes for baked hams.

OKRA

This homely pod can be slimy, and many varieties are a bit fuzzy, but stew it with tomatoes and shrimp (prawns), or fry it in a crisp coating of cornmeal, and all is forgiven. Pickled with hot peppers and com-mercially packaged in jars, it makes a startling garnish for Bloody Marys, Louisiana style. Okra was probably introduced to the Americas by African slaves, who carried the seeds from their homeland. Known in the Bantu language as *gumbo,* it thickens and flavors the Creole stew by the same name.

TABASCO

The diamond-shaped Tabasco logo is one of the best-known labels in the world, printed in Chinese, Dutch, English, French, Italian, Japanese, and Swedish for fans in more than one hundred countries. The pepper fields and brewery are located on Avery Island, the tip of an underwater salt dome. It provides salt for the Tabasco chile mash, which is fermented and aged in oak barrels for up to three years, then mixed with vinegar and set aside for another month before it's strained and bottled. The company is still run by the family of Edmund McIlhenny, who established the brand in 1868.

STEEN'S PURE CANE SYRUP   PRALINES   CHICORY COFFEE

HUBIG'S PIES

Like the label says, pies from the downtown bakery of the Simon Hubig Company are "made fresh locally." The thick-crusted turnovers are strictly nonpartisan, high in both fat and carbs, deep-fried, and coated in a sugary glaze. Sheathed in little paper envelopes, they're the traditional handheld desserts offered at walk-up sandwich counters, seafood markets, neighborhood sweets shops, and Carnival picnics. They're even sold in hardware stores. Most New Orleans schoolkids can name a favorite flavor: lemon, apple, chocolate, coconut, peach, pineapple, or sweet potato.

STEEN'S PURE CANE SYRUP

Steen's Pure Cane Syrup, similar to molasses but thinner and slightly milder in flavor, is a by-product of the sugar-refining process. Since 1910, the tangy sweetener has been sealed in bright yellow cans at a small sugarcane mill in Abbeville, Louisiana, and it still remains a sentimental favorite statewide, perfect for drizzling over biscuits, pancakes, and the Creole rice fritters known as calas (page 174). Steen's also produces molasses, as well as a trendy cane vinegar fermented from pure sugarcane juice.

PRALINES

The signature sweet of New Orleans is sold in the praline shops of the French Quarter, which ship their wares around the world. Often the kitchens are open to view, so customers can watch the hot candy being ladled onto marble slabs to cool. Several variations have been concocted over the years (chocolate, coconut, rum), but the original version—a simple blend of brown sugar, cream, butter, and pecans—is still the best. The native pecan was substituted for almonds or hazelnuts, traditional in European-style pralines, by French and Spanish colonists who introduced these to Louisiana.

CHICORY COFFEE

Roasted and ground chicory root, an herb related to the thistle, was used to stretch coffee rations during the Civil War and other times when coffee was difficult to obtain. Eventually residents of southern Louisiana developed a taste for the rich and fragrant brew of chicory and coffee, now packaged as "New Orleans blend" and served throughout the city. Waiters may ask if you want "chicory or regular" (pure coffee). Either way, the coffee is often dark French roast and served very strong. Local custom dictates that it be poured into the cup simultaneously with steamed milk for café au lait.

Much of the local diet originates underwater in New Orleans, a salty old city squeezed between the Mississippi River and wide, scenic Lake Pontchartrain, crisscrossed by bayous, surrounded by swamps, and a quick sail away from the Gulf of Mexico.

SEAFOOD

Early French colonists called south Louisiana *le flotant,* "the floating land," as it is caught in a vast net of waterways and inlets created over thousands of years as sediment worked its way down the Mississippi River to various outlets in the Gulf of Mexico. Today Louisiana lays claim to more than 40 percent of the nation's coastal wetlands, rich natural breeding grounds that consistently place it among the top American producers of shrimp (prawns), oysters, blue crabs, and various finfish. More than twenty thousand residents earn all or part of their income from commercial fishing, an economic wave that sends ripples through dozens of other industries, from boat building and repair, to processing and wholesaling, to restaurants and tourism.

Once the stuff of shudders, crawfish, alligators, and turtles are now farmed to meet the demands of regional chefs and home cooks, as well as an ever-growing national market. Aquaculture has also made catfish and soft-shell crabs both abundant and inexpensive. Even in the middle of New Orleans, behind the walls of Orleans Parish Prison, inmates and staff cultivate their own supply of tilapia, better known as St. Peter's fish, a major food source for centuries in Africa and Asia.

Finfish harvested wild from the Gulf of Mexico are listed on chalkboards at seafood shops and restaurants. Gulf mackerel, also known as Spanish mackerel, is rich and tasty, an excellent source of omega-3 fatty acids. Amberjack is prized for its sweet, firm flesh. Blackfin tuna is full flavored and meaty. Mahimahi is a more marketable name for a type of dolphin that is not a mammal. Its dark flesh turns white when cooked, with firm, large flakes and a mildly sweet flavor. All are especially well suited to the grill.

Yet despite this vast array of local seafood, natives and visitors are most likely to order the big three: shrimp, crabs, and oysters. A typical feast at a waterfront seafood house begins with spicy boiled shellfish or shrimp rémoulade (page 73), or maybe an icy tray of raw oysters on the half shell, before moving on to massive platters piled high with crisp-fried shrimp, oysters, soft-shell crabs, and stuffed crabs. All call for plenty of ice-cold draft beer, preferably Dixie or Abita, both locally brewed. And it's never a chore to eat your vegetables: Plates are generally garnished with French fries, a few shreds of iceberg lettuce, one paper-thin tomato slice, and a couple of dill pickle chips.

Shrimp, crabs, and oysters may be delicacies, but are everyday fare in Louisiana.

Belly up to the bar for fresh local oysters. A cool dozen will be presented in moments by expert shuckers at classic seafood houses and oyster bars all over town, where several generations of New Orleanians have enjoyed their "ersters" raw or cooked— whether fried, broiled, barbecued, or stewed.

Seafood on the Menu

Great old oyster bars include Acme Oyster House or Felix's in the French Quarter, The Pearl in the Central Business District, and Casamento's Uptown. Bruning's Sea Food Restaurant has been a lakefront favorite for nearly 150 years. Other good choices are Sid-Mar's in Bucktown, Mandina's in Mid-City, and Cooter Brown's or Franky and Johnny's Uptown. Uglesich's, open for lunch in the Central Business District, serves exquisite raw and fried oysters and shrimp (prawns).

Backyard Seafood Fry

A backyard seafood fry is down-home entertaining at its best, promising tall tales, an abundance of decadent foods, and hands-on dining. In New Orleans and coastal Louisiana, the kettle is usually stocked with fresh soft-shell crabs, plump oysters, or Gulf shrimp (prawns). Farm-raised catfish is also popular, though aficionados swear by wild "flathead cat" from the Mississippi River. Thick batters or elaborate coatings are rare. Southern-fried seafood is simply dusted with cornmeal or corn flour, usually seasoned with plenty of salt and black pepper plus a bit of cayenne, then fried in hot peanut oil.

The main dish of fried seafood is typically accompanied by a regular cast of side dishes, such as crispy hush puppies, tangy coleslaw, creamy potato salad, fresh buttered corn on the cob, and cheese grits spiked with plenty of cayenne pepper. Ice chests are stocked with bottles of locally brewed beer and root beer. Large pitchers are filled with frosty cold lemonade and sweetened iced tea, while desserts typically range from juicy peach cobbler to chilled wedges of watermelon.

Shucking Oysters

OPENING THE SHELL First, scrub the oysters with a stiff brush under cold running water. Using a rubber mitt made for shucking oysters or a tough work glove to protect your hand, place an oyster in the palm of your hand. Using a proper oyster knife (never a kitchen knife, which is too flexible and almost certain to cause injury), gently insert the blade into the gap between the top and bottom halves at the hinge end. Pointing the blade away from you, in case the knife slips, firmly twist the handle until the halves separate.

RELEASING THE OYSTER Gently slide the blade between the two shells to sever the adductor muscle that connects them near the hinge. Discard the shallow top shell. Finally, work the blade under the oyster to release it from the muscle that connects it to the bottom shell, taking care not to cut into the meat or lose the briny "liquor."

SERVING Use the knife to scrape away any bits of debris clinging to the shell or the meat. Serve the oysters in their bottom shells, atop a bed of ice.

BLUE CRABS

SHRIMP

REDFISH

CRAWFISH

BLUE CRABS

Their official designation, *Callinectes sapidus,* means "savory beautiful swimmer," and they are, with graceful back paddles and a turquoise-tinted shell that inspired the common name. Blue crabs are harvested year-round in traps set in the brackish waters of Louisiana's inlets, bayous, and rivers. They're boiled while still alive, then served whole for casual meals. Jumbo lump crabmeat, which comes from the back fins, is used for sautés and gratins. The coarser claw meat goes into stuffed crabs.

SHRIMP

By far the most popular shellfish in the state, shrimp (prawns) have been a vital ingredient in Creole and Cajun cuisine for centuries, prepared in hundreds of ways. The two main types fished commercially in Louisiana are white shrimp, considered the premium catch, and brown shrimp, which are slightly firmer and harder to peel. Around inland bayous, brown shrimp are in season from May through July, and white shrimp from August through mid-January, but both are harvested year-round in deeper offshore waters of the Gulf.

REDFISH

The Cajun blackening craze of the 1980s introduced Louisiana redfish to the world, but beneath the rosy skin and trademark black dot on the tail, it's nearly indistinguishable from humbler (and less expensive) cousins in the drum family. Also found in the Gulf of Mexico, black drum is just as mild and flaky. Known to some as croakers, drum are named for the deep vibrating sounds they emit during mating season. All are fine for the sauté pan or grill, as well as for Creole-style courtbouillon (page 120), stew, or bouillabaisse.

CRAWFISH

Louisiana is Crawfish Capital of the World, a title that remains unchallenged, even though the humble "mudbugs" are slowly gaining favor across the country. The texture and sweet flavor are reminiscent of lobster, which they resemble in miniature, averaging four inches (ten centimeters) in length, with curled-under tails and tiny claws. They are the premier icon of Cajun cookery, served boiled, étoufféed, stewed, and baked into pies. Cleaned soft-shell crawfish are fried, as are the tails, known as Cajun popcorn.

CATFISH

OYSTERS

POMPANO

SOFT-SHELL CRABS

CATFISH

Named for the whiskerlike feelers that hang around its mouth, the catfish is an old Southern favorite with a steadily growing profile on the national culinary scene, primarily due to mass production at commercial farms. Several species are also harvested wild in the fresh waters of Louisiana, including blue cat, channel cat, and flathead catfish. The first choice for community fish fries, the sweet white fillets are also stewed in spicy Creole sauces or sautéed with toasted pecans.

OYSTERS

The creamy-textured bivalves cultivated and harvested wild in Louisiana, known as Eastern or Atlantic oysters, are commonly served raw or fried, but they are also savored in gumbos, soups, stuffings, and such extravaganzas as oysters Rockefeller (page 74). Thanks to modern refrigeration, they're safely consumed even during months without an *r*, but they are at their plump and briny peak during fall and winter. (Their meat becomes soft and milky during summer spawning.)

POMPANO

Mild-flavored and succulent pompano, a choice member of the jack family, is one of the most prized catches in the Gulf of Mexico. It is best known in New Orleans as the star of *pompano en papillote*, a classic Creole dish originally created at Antoine's during the nineteenth century to honor a visiting French balloonist. For the celebrated dish, an envelope of parchment puffs up like a balloon around the delicate white fillet, thus steaming the fish in a rich cream sauce with lump crabmeat and shrimp (prawns).0

SOFT-SHELL CRABS

A blue crab must occasionally shed its shell in order to grow. Underneath is a leathery new shell that allows the creature inside to stretch before the shell hardens again, an event that takes just a few hours in its natural environment. If a crab is captured during this brief window and placed on ice to suspend the hardening of the shell, the soft-shell crab can then be cleaned, battered, and fried for one of the great Louisiana delicacies. Thanks to modern aquaculture, producers can now control those conditions for a guaranteed harvest.

Even fast foods are taken seriously in Louisiana, where hot boudin is sold in gas stations and scruffy neighborhood po-boy joints endure for generations. Coffee and doughnuts translates into café au lait and beignets, pralines are still made by hand, and snowball stands offer at least fifty flavors.

LOCAL FAST FOOD

Popeye's Famous Fried Chicken was born in New Orleans, and the suburbs are alight with other drive-through chains, but most natives who want to eat in a hurry prefer the small, local eateries that offer a garlicky roast beef po-boy dripping gravy and mayonnaise, or a massive "peacemaker" of crisp fried oysters and shrimp (prawns) heaped inside a loaf of butter-toasted French bread. The city's best po-boys, served either hot or cold, can be found at Parasol's and Domilise's Uptown, Mother's in the Central Business District, and R&O on the lakefront in Bucktown.

Bucktown is also the place to pick up a bag of spicy boiled shrimp (prawns), crawfish, or crabs for a waterfront picnic. Area seafood markets, such as Schaefer & Rusich or Deanies, also sell the essential saltines, boiled new potatoes and corn, and rolls of paper towels. To outfit a similar feast under moss-draped oaks, stop at K-Jean's near City Park.

Nearly every neighborhood has a snowball stand. Hansen's Sno-Bliz on Tchoupitoulas Street still uses the ice-shaving machine that Ernest Hansen built in 1939, packing the fluffy white powder into containers ranging from small cups to full-sized garbage cans (convenient for daiquiri parties at nearby Tulane University). Chinese-food cartons are the signature vessels at Plum Street Snowball Stand, a landmark for more than 60 years.

Street vendors have always colored the local landscape. The beloved Roman Candy wagon, a mule-drawn taffy kitchen on wheels, has made its wobbly rounds Uptown and Downtown since 1915. On Bourbon Street you can still bite into Lucky Dogs from one of the surreal wiener-shaped carts immortalized in John Kennedy Toole's well-known comic novel, *A Confederacy of Dunces.*

Eva Perry earned her reputation selling homemade sweets from a handbasket, working downtown office buildings and the corridors of City Hall. Now she has her own walk-up stand on Magazine Street, Tee-Eva's World Famous Pies and Pralines, where you can also get a quick fix of home-style jambalaya or red beans. Another great source for Creole pecan candies is Old Town Praline Shop, located in the French Quarter.

Angelo Brocato's Ice Cream and Confectionery on Carrollton Avenue is a vintage shrine for fresh fruit ices, gelati, and Sicilian pastries. Spumoni comes in wedges of extravagantly layered pastels, and the lemon ice is wonderfully tart and refreshing, a perfect antidote to the local climate.

The food might be fast but this busy city makes sure it still tastes delicious.

It may be called a po-boy, but the king of New Orleans sandwiches is a two-fisted feast on French bread, piled high and messy with anything from your basic ham and cheese to fried soft-shell crabs. Order a cold draft or root beer, grab a bag of chips, and roll up your sleeves.

Po-Boy Bread

Good-quality French bread has been an essential part of the New Orleans diet for generations. Crackly on the outside and light and airy on the inside, it leaves a trail of crumbs across restaurants and kitchens. A must for po-boy sandwiches, it's also the traditional accompaniment for red beans, gumbo, and other slow-pot specialties. Yard-long loaves, usually peeking above their paper wrappers, bear such venerable logos as Reisings, Leidenheimer, and Alois J. Binder.

Po-Boy: The Legend

Other cities have their hoagies and subs, which are similar in shape and size, but are still miles away from the authentic po-boy, with its ethereal French bread, perfectly fried seafood, or slow-roasted meats.

According to legend, the name dates back to a local transportation strike during the 1920s, when union members were treated to free sandwiches at a deli owned by former streetcar conductors Bennie and Clovis Martin. Whenever a striker approached the counter, Bennie would yell to Clovis, "Here comes another poor boy!"

Today almost every neighborhood has its own po-boy joint, sometimes within a corner grocery or bar, and usually staffed by a harried cook and waitress with very little patience for newcomers who don't get the lingo. You mainly need to know that "brown gravy" is roast beef gravy, "red gravy" is marinara sauce, "MY-nez" is mayonnaise, and "hot sausage" is fiery with cayenne pepper. You'll also be asked if you want the sandwich "dressed," that is, with shredded lettuce, tomato slices, dill pickles, and my-nez.

Making a Po-Boy

PREPARING THE BREAD Although light and crisp New Orleans–style French bread is best for po-boys, you may substitute a French baguette, seeded Italian loaf, or crusty roll. The traditional length for a sandwich is eight to ten inches. Split the bread lengthwise, butter it lightly, and broil it, cut sides up, until the surface is toasted to a golden brown but the bread is still soft.

FILLING THE SANDWICH Generously spread both halves with Creole mustard or any other spicy brown mustard and mayonnaise. Pile on the filling of your choice. Traditional favorites are roast beef and gravy, fried oysters, fried shrimp (prawns), hot Italian sausage, meatballs and mozzarella, or ham and Swiss cheese.

DRESSING THE SANDWICH Top the meat or seafood with finely shredded lettuce or cabbage, thinly sliced tomatoes, and slices of dill pickle. Serve the po-boy with potato chips and an ice-cold draft or root beer.

Here in sugarcane country, where a civilized meal can last for hours, dessert will be served at least once. Afternoon visitors are often greeted with coffee and cake, and the table of homemade sweets runneth over at every church supper and family reunion.

DESSERTS

Perhaps that old expression should be changed to "as American as pecan pie," to celebrate the indigenous nut that crowns the sweetest of Southern desserts. Another New World native, sweet potatoes, adds its natural sugars and autumn color to pies popular throughout Louisiana. Spring brings Ruston peaches and Ponchatoula strawberries for shortcakes and cobblers. Late summer is fig season, when backyard harvests go into pies, cakes, preserves, and, the most anticipated treat of all, fig ice cream. In fact, ice cream is always welcome in the steamy subtropical climate. Old-fashioned "frozen custard" (aka French vanilla ice cream) is layered with crumbled pralines for gold-streaked parfaits. Frozen cream cheese, enriched by the locally produced Creole cream cheese, makes a tangy bed for Louisiana blackberries.

Fresh from the bakery, yard-long loaves of French bread are perfect for po-boys, but by the second day the brittle crust and airy interior are already too hard for sandwiches. However, they are just right for soaking up a rich and spicy custard to create a bread pudding. Usually draped in a whiskey-laced sauce, it's the signature dessert of New Orleans, from a simple dish served at mom's kitchen table to the famous bread pudding soufflé at Commander's Palace.

Thin slices from a day-old loaf also make fine French toast, now served as a dessert at stylish restaurants such as Gabrielle, where pastry chef Mary Sonnier tops her butter-sizzled *pain perdu* (lost bread) with ripe, juicy strawberries and whipped cream. Generations of Louisiana children have helped themselves to the even more rustic treat known as a

French bread float, created by pulling the fluff from a crusty end piece, then buttering the hollowed "nose" and filling it with Steen's Cane Syrup. Similar to molasses, the dark sugarcane sweetener also colors an old-fashioned country cake known as *gâteau de sirop*, a Cajun-style gingerbread baked in a cast-iron frying pan.

Birthdays and other festive occasions call for a doberge cake (pronounced DOE-bash in New Orleans), probably descended from the Austrian Dobos torte. Eight or nine thin layers of genoise sponge cake are spread with buttercream or custard filling, then stacked into a round cake and coated with a hard glaze. A standard at most local bakeries, it is a specialty of the citywide Gambino's chain. Many flavors are available, but chocolate and lemon are the most common.

Enough is never enough in Louisiana, where dessert is part of every meal.

Brennan's created bananas Foster in 1951 for a *Holiday* magazine feature. Little did anyone imagine that the flaming dessert would become the most requested dish at Brennan's, which now sets fire to some thirty-five thousand pounds (seventeen thousand kilograms) of bananas each year.

Crêpes Fitzgerald

Former Brennan's chef Paul Blangé originated many of the signature dishes that are still on the menu at the Royal Street landmark today, including bananas Foster. Blangé named another fiery dessert for a party of six businessmen from Fitzgerald Advertising who lunched at Brennan's every day for years, always at the same table. Crêpes Fitzgerald are filled with sour cream and cream cheese, then flamed with fresh sliced strawberries in maraschino liqueur.

Flaming Desserts

Flaming desserts were once the crowning glory of haute cuisine and, although now viewed as charmingly retro and a little kitschy, they still add plenty of flash to the historic dining rooms of New Orleans. At Antoine's the flaming football-shaped baked Alaska serves two, and, with advance notice, it may be emblazoned with a personal message. The city's oldest restaurant also sets light to buttery, orange-scented crêpes Suzette and classic cherries jubilee. At Broussard's, the eponymous crêpes Broussard are rolled around cream cheese and pecans, then ignited with brandy in a strawberry sauce. At Emeril's Delmonico the crêpes Suzette gets "kicked up a notch" with citrus chocolate ice cream, and the chocolate-hazelnut baked Alaska is fired in a Frangelico rum sauce.

Still, Brennan's original creation remains the most famous of all the French Creole flambéed desserts. It is now served at countless other restaurants, locally and nationwide, and has inspired such spin-offs as bananas Foster pie, shortcake, waffles, and ice cream.

Preparing Bananas Foster

HEATING THE SAUCE There's always a sense of drama in the dining rooms at Brennan's when a waiter wheels out the cart for tableside preparation of the restaurant's famous Bananas Foster. He empties small dishes of butter, brown sugar, and ground cinnamon into a flambé pan, then heats it over a low flame, tipping and swirling the pan until the butter melts and the sugar dissolves.

FLAMING THE BANANAS Next he adds a shot of banana liqueur along with quartered bananas. Just as the bananas are starting to brown, he adds dark rum and tips the pan to ignite the alcohol. Sometimes the flames are so spectacular that nearby diners gasp and lean away while the waiter ladles the sauce in high arcs until the flames extinguish on their own.

SERVING THE DESSERT For each diner, the waiter arranges three or four pieces of banana on top of a bowl of French vanilla ice cream and finishes the dessert with a generous drizzle of the warm sauce. The show ends with fragrant cups of dark French roast coffee.

APPETIZERS AND FIRST COURSES

Dining in New Orleans is leisurely, and most meals begin with

Sid-Mar's OF BUCKTOWN RESTAURANT & BAR

BERNICE'S

a few savory bites to tease the appetite and start the conversation.

Portabello
$1.25 each

Oyster
1/4 lb. $2.00
/2 lb. $4.00
$8.00

New Orleanians love to share food, so it is not uncommon for a group to order an assortment of appetizers for the table. In casual restaurants, the main course is traditionally preceded by stuffed artichokes, crisp onion rings, or icy trays of raw oysters. In grander surroundings, it might be oysters Rockefeller or shrimp rémoulade. Stylish new bistros encourage guests to make a meal of two or three savory "small plates." When entertaining at home, busy cooks often rely on boiled shrimp or marinated crab claws from the neighborhood seafood market, or assemble a colorful platter of antipasti from a Sicilian deli.

CREOLE TOMATO TART WITH HERB CRUST

Always cause for celebration, the arrival of the first Creole tomatoes of the season, which begins as early as March and peaks from May to June, is ushered in with marching bands at the old French Market. Following in early June, the annual French Market Tomato Festival features food booths and cooking demonstrations by local chefs. The locally grown beauties are prized for their sweet flavor. This simple tart lets their unique taste shine through, although it could also be topped with any variety of vine-ripened tomato—or even heaped with hothouse cherry tomatoes to brighten a winter day.

1 To make the pastry, in a food processor, combine the flour, Parmesan, rosemary, salt, and pepper and process for about 30 seconds to mix and chop the rosemary. Cut the butter into 8 pieces and distribute the pieces evenly over the flour mixture. Pulse about 10 times, or until the mixture resembles coarse meal. Sprinkle the ice water over the surface and pulse about 7 more times. The dough will still appear rather loose, but should hold together when pressed between your fingers. Shape the dough into a disk ¾ inch (2 cm) thick, wrap tightly in plastic wrap, and refrigerate for at least 30 minutes or up to overnight.

2 Preheat the oven to 425°F (220°C). On a lightly floured work surface, roll out the dough into an evenly thick round, about 12 inches (30 cm) in diameter and ⅛ inch (3 mm) thick. Roll the round loosely around the pin, then carefully unroll it into a 9- or 10-inch (23- or 25-cm) tart pan with a removable bottom, allowing the excess to drape over the sides. Press the pastry gently into the bottom and sides of the pan, then roll the pin across the top of the pan, trimming off the excess dough.

3 Prick the pastry evenly over the bottom with fork tines, then line with a sheet of parchment (baking) paper or aluminum foil. Fill the pastry with pie weights or dried beans and bake until the pastry has set, about

8 minutes. Remove the pie weights and parchment, return the pastry to the oven, and continue to bake until the pastry is tender and golden, 8–12 minutes longer. Transfer to a wire rack and let cool completely.

4 To make the filling, in a food processor, combine the goat cheese, 2 tablespoons of the chopped basil, and ¼ teaspoon pepper. Process until smooth, about 30 seconds.

5 Spread the cheese mixture evenly over the cooled crust. Beginning at the outer edge, arrange the tomato slices in slightly overlapping concentric circles on top of the cheese mixture (save the end pieces of the tomatoes for another purpose). Drizzle lightly with olive oil and sprinkle with coarse salt and pepper and the remaining 1 tablespoon chopped basil. Garnish the center of the tart with the basil sprig and serve at once.

Serve with an herbal white wine such as Sancerre or Pouilly-Fumé.

FOR THE PASTRY

1½ cups (7½ oz/235 g) all-purpose (plain) flour

2 tablespoons freshly grated Parmesan cheese

1 tablespoon fresh rosemary leaves

½ teaspoon fine sea salt

¼ teaspoon freshly ground pepper

½ cup (4 oz/125 g) chilled unsalted butter

3 tablespoons ice water

FOR THE FILLING

¼ lb (125 g) fresh goat cheese

3 tablespoons chopped fresh basil, plus 1 sprig for garnish

Freshly ground pepper

4 ripe tomatoes, such as Creole or beefsteak, cut into slices ¼ inch (6 mm) thick

Extra-virgin olive oil for drizzling

Coarse sea salt for sprinkling

Makes 6 servings

FRENCH-FRIED EGGPLANT

Crisp and light, these ethereal fritters bear no resemblance to the baskets of sodden, overseasoned vegetables that many bars serve. New Orleans–style fried eggplant has been offered with cocktails in the city's grandest restaurants and homes for generations, usually with an incongruent (but oddly compatible) sprinkling of confectioners' sugar, although grated Parmesan is another option. Eggplant fritters are traditional, but the same batter and technique could also be used with other vegetables, such as whole mushrooms, zucchini (courgette) slices, or bell pepper (capsicum) rings.

1 eggplant (aubergine) about
½ lb (250 g), peeled

Sea salt

Peanut oil for deep frying

FOR THE BATTER

1 cup (5 oz/155 g) all-purpose
(plain) flour

½ teaspoon baking powder

½ teaspoon sea salt

¼ teaspoon freshly ground
white pepper

1 large egg

1 cup (8 fl oz/250 ml) whole milk

1 tablespoon peanut oil

Confectioners' (icing) sugar
for dusting

Makes 6 servings

1 Cut the eggplant lengthwise into slices ½ inch (12 mm) thick, then cut the slices into sticks ½ inch (12 mm) wide and 4 inches (10 cm) long (about the size of steak fries). Generously salt the eggplant sticks, tossing to coat them well. Set aside in a colander to drain for about 30 minutes.

2 Preheat the oven to 200°F (95°C). Pour oil to a depth of 2 inches (5 cm) into a deep, heavy saucepan or a deep fryer and heat to to 360°F (182°C) on a deep-frying thermometer. A thermometer is essential to maintain the correct temperature for the lightest results. Line an ovenproof platter with several layers of paper towel and set it near the stove.

3 To make the batter, in a bowl, whisk together the flour, baking powder, salt, and white pepper until thoroughly combined. Add the egg, milk, and oil and whisk to blend.

4 Rinse the eggplant sticks with cool running water and pat dry thoroughly. Working in batches, dip the eggplant sticks into the batter, coating well, then lift out, shaking off the excess. Carefully slip into the hot oil and fry, turning once, until crisp and golden brown, 2–3 minutes. Using a slotted spoon, transfer to the paper towels to drain. Repeat with the remaining eggplant sticks, always making sure the oil returns to 360°F (182°C) before adding the next batch. Keep warm in the oven until all the eggplant is fried.

5 Pile the eggplant sticks on a platter and, using a fine-mesh sieve, dust with confectioners' sugar. Serve at once.

Serve with tall, icy mint juleps, as eggplant partners well with mint.

MIXED SEAFOOD RÉMOULADE

Inspired by the classic French sauce but more piquant, New Orleans–style rémoulade is often spiked with zesty Creole mustard (page 48), a cross between whole-grain and smooth brown varieties. Recipes for rémoulade fall into one of two broad categories: white or red. This recipe is for a red rémoulade, that is, it contains no mayonnaise. It is traditionally tossed with boiled shrimp and the mixture piled atop a bed of crisp iceberg lettuce. The sauce may be refrigerated for up to a week before the seafood is added.

1 To make the rémoulade, in a food processor, combine the green onions, celery, parsley, and garlic and pulse until finely chopped. Scrape down the sides of the processor bowl and add the mustard, vinegar, paprika, and horseradish. With the machine running, slowly pour the olive oil through the feed tube and process until a smooth emulsion forms. Use a rubber spatula to scrape the dressing into a large nonreactive bowl. Season to taste with salt and pepper and stir in the capers. Set aside for 1 hour at room temperature to allow the flavors to blend.

2 Pick over the crabmeat to remove any bits of shell. Add the shrimp and crabmeat to the dressing. Toss gently until the seafood is evenly coated, being careful not to break up the lumps of crabmeat. Cover in an airtight container and refrigerate for 2–3 hours to chill well and allow the flavors to blend.

3 Taste and adjust the seasoning. Divide the shredded lettuce evenly among chilled salad plates and mound the seafood on top of the lettuce. Peel and quarter the hard-boiled eggs. Garnish each plate with 2 egg quarters and a wedge of lemon and serve.

Serve with a demi-sec Champagne to complement the seafood and balance the zesty sauce.

FOR THE RÉMOULADE

4 green (spring) onions, white and pale green parts, coarsely chopped

1 celery stalk, coarsely chopped

⅓ cup (⅓ oz/10 g) loosely packed fresh flat-leaf (Italian) parsley

1 clove garlic, chopped

2 tablespoons Creole mustard or coarse-brown mustard

2 tablespoons tarragon vinegar or white wine vinegar

1 tablespoon sweet paprika

1 teaspoon prepared horseradish, or more to taste

6 tablespoons (3 fl oz/90 ml) extra-virgin olive oil

Sea salt and freshly ground pepper

2 tablespoons capers

1 lb (500 g) lump crabmeat or crawfish tails

1 lb (500 g) peeled and deveined cooked shrimp (prawns)

8 cups (1½ lb/750 g) shredded iceberg lettuce

4 hard-boiled eggs

8 lemon wedges

Makes 8 servings

Crawfish Farms

Louisiana supplies around 95 percent of the commercial crawfish available in the United States—and consumes 90 percent of them. Much of the wild crawfish harvest comes from the picturesque Atchafalaya Swamp, a drainage basin for the Mississippi River and the nation's largest undeveloped wetland.

Thanks to modern aquaculture, crawfish farming has become an important industry in southern Louisiana and east Texas. Some growers flood fallow rice fields in October to make way for this secondary crop, while others build levees around marshes to create massive ponds. The flooded fields or ponds are stocked once with the crustaceans, which then multiply on their own, surviving on grasses and other feed. When the land is pumped dry each spring, the crawfish burrow into the mud to lay eggs. One female may produce as many as eight hundred eggs per year.

Live crawfish are available from December until July and most plentiful in spring. Peeled, frozen tail meat is available year-round, ready for a quick crawfish pie, étouffée, bisque, or stew.

CRAB ROCKEFELLER

Oysters Rockefeller, crowned by a money-green sauce as rich as its namesake, was created in the late 1890s at Antoine's Restaurant, where the original recipe remains top secret. Similar versions, however, are available at most other shrines of classic New Orleans cuisine, including Brennan's, which contributed this variation created by sous-chef Lazone Randolph. Here he replaces the oysters with lump crabmeat, but the traditional sauce remains the same, colored by a blend of anise liqueur and herbs; it is not, contrary to some attempts to re-create the dish, prepared with spinach.

1 cup (8 oz/250 g) unsalted butter

1 small celery stalk, preferably from the heart, finely chopped

6 green (spring) onions, including tender green parts, finely chopped

½ cup (¾ oz/20 g) minced fresh flat-leaf (Italian) parsley

1½ tablespoons Worcestershire sauce

½ teaspoon Tabasco

¼ cup (2 fl oz/60 ml) Herbsaint (page 35) or Pernod

½ cup (2 oz/60 g) fine dried bread crumbs, preferably from French bread

Sea salt and freshly ground pepper

1 lb (500 g) lump crabmeat, picked over to remove any bits of shell

Makes 6 servings

1 In a frying pan over medium-high heat, melt the butter. Add the celery, green onions, and parsley and sauté just until tender, 3–5 minutes. Reduce the heat to medium-low, stir in the Worcestershire and Tabasco, and continue cooking for 10 minutes to blend the flavors. Add the liqueur and bread crumbs and cook for 5 minutes longer to blend. Season to taste with salt and pepper. Transfer to a covered bowl and refrigerate until set but not hard, about 1 hour.

2 Preheat the oven to 375°F (190°C). Lightly butter 6 shallow ramekins or small baking dishes and divide the crabmeat among them, reserving 6 of the largest pieces for garnish.

3 Remove the sauce from the refrigerator. Using an electric mixer on medium speed, beat the sauce until it is lighter in texture and aerated, about 2 minutes. Spoon 3–4 tablespoons of the sauce over the crabmeat in each of the ramekins, and garnish each ramekin with a piece of the reserved crab. Bake until the topping is puffed and lightly browned, about 10 minutes. Serve at once.

Serve with a dry Champagne or a full-flavored white Burgundy.

Variation: For oysters Rockefeller, have ready 2 dozen scrubbed, freshly shucked oysters on the half shell (see page 53). After beating the sauce, scrape it into a pastry bag fitted with a large plain tip. Cover the bottoms of 6 shallow baking dishes with rock salt (to hold the oysters steady) and place 4 oysters on the half shell in each dish. Alternatively, cover the bottom of a large rimmed baking sheet with rock salt and place all of the oysters in the baking sheet. Pipe 1 tablespoon of the sauce over each oyster. Bake in a pre-heated 375°F (190°C) oven until puffed and lightly browned, 5–8 minutes. Serve at once.

CRAWFISH BEIGNETS

Unlike the airy, pillow-shaped beignets made famous by sidewalk cafés in the French Quarter, these country cousins are rounder and just a bit rough, with a springy texture similar to cake doughnuts. Beignets, also known as croquignoles, are usually sweet, drizzled with cane syrup or molasses. In this case, however, they are savory snacks studded with chopped crawfish, for a cross between hush puppies and conch fritters. For a piquant dipping sauce, blend equal parts mayonnaise and Creole mustard.

1 In a bowl, whisk together the flour, sugar, baking powder, baking soda, celery salt, and cayenne until thoroughly combined. Set aside.

2 Preheat the oven to 200°F (95°C). Pour oil to a depth of 2 inches (5 cm) into a heavy saucepan or a deep fryer and heat to 350°F (180°C) on a deep-frying thermometer. A thermometer is essential to maintain the correct temperature for the lightest results. Line a platter with several layers of paper towels and set it near the stove.

3 Meanwhile, in a separate bowl, whisk together the egg and buttermilk until blended. When the oil is hot, make a well in the center of the flour mixture and pour in the wet ingredients, stirring just until blended. Fold in the crawfish, green onions, bell pepper, and parsley. Season to taste with salt and black pepper. The batter must be mixed just before frying for the beignets to rise properly as they cook.

4 Working in batches, drop the batter by rounded teaspoonfuls into the hot oil, being careful not to crowd the pan. Fry, turning once, until crisp and golden brown, 2–3 minutes. The beignets should turn over by themselves as they cook; if they don't, give them a gentle push with a long-handled fork or chopstick. Using a slotted spoon, transfer to the paper towels to drain. Repeat with the remaining batter, always making sure the oil returns to 350°F (180°C) before adding the next batch. Keep warm in the oven until all of the beignets are fried. Serve at once.

Serve with a light lager or pale ale.

1 cup (5 oz/155 g) all-purpose (plain) flour

1 tablespoon sugar

1 teaspoon baking powder

¼ teaspoon baking soda (bicarbonate of soda)

¼ teaspoon celery salt

⅛ teaspoon cayenne pepper

Peanut oil for deep-frying

1 large egg

½ cup (4 fl oz/125 ml) buttermilk

½ lb (250 g) cooked crawfish tails, peeled and deveined shrimp (prawns), or lump crabmeat, coarsely chopped

2 green (spring) onions, including tender green parts, minced

¼ cup (1½ oz/45 g) seeded and minced red bell pepper (capsicum)

2 tablespoons minced fresh flat-leaf (Italian) parsley

Sea salt and freshly ground black pepper

Makes 2 dozen beignets

Abita Beer

The shady little town of Abita Springs, about thirty miles north of New Orleans, is famed for its piney woods and artesian water. In the days before air-conditioning, it was a summer resort where city dwellers could escape the heat and yellow fever epidemics. And even before the first European explorers arrived, it was a haven for native Choctaws, who named it Abita, or "healing waters."

Today it's best known as the source of bottled Abita Springs water and the premier regional beer. The Abita Brewing Company, established in 1986, has grown from an annual output of fifteen hundred barrels to more than forty thousand. The small-batch lagers and ales are cold filtered and made from a blend of malted barley, yeast, hops, and water that is drawn from an aquifer eighteen hundred feet (six hundred meters) below ground. Popular standards like mellow Abita Amber and malty Turbo Dog are supplemented by seasonal offerings, as well as sugarcane-sweetened Abita root beer. A good match for crawfish beignets and other spicy fare, the beers can be found in bottles and on tap in most area restaurants.

WARM LOUISIANA GREENS SALAD WITH SMOKED MUSHROOMS

The Louisiana country standard "mess of greens" would ordinarily be cooked with chunks of slab bacon. While out with the garden basket, the cook might also forage around for some wild mushrooms. This dish goes uptown at the Crescent City Farmers' Market (page 19), a lively outdoor market that convenes at various locations around New Orleans, providing an opportunity for city dwellers to do some foraging of their own. The market's comanager, Kristen Essig, contributed this salad, which preserves the fresh flavor of the field greens while replacing the bacon with olive oil and meaty smoked shiitakes.

FOR THE VINAIGRETTE

1½ tablespoons minced shallots

2 teaspoons Creole mustard (page 48) or coarse-grain brown mustard

1 teaspoon wildflower honey

1½ tablespoons Champagne vinegar

¼ cup (2 fl oz/60 ml) extra-virgin olive oil

FOR THE SALAD

½ lb (250 g) shiitake mushrooms

5 cups (6–7 oz/185–220 g) firmly packed, assorted young Louisiana greens such as baby Swiss chard, baby purple mustard greens, mizuna, spinach, or young red kale

½ red onion, thinly sliced

Sea salt and freshly ground pepper

¼ lb (125 g) aged cheese such as Parmesan or *grana padano*, for shaving

Makes 4 servings

1 To make the vinaigrette, in a small nonreactive bowl combine the shallots, mustard, and honey. Whisk in the vinegar to combine. Slowly add the olive oil in a steady stream, whisking constantly until emulsified. Set aside.

2 To smoke the mushrooms, prepare a stove-top smoker according to the manufacturer's directions. Trim the mushroom stems, then wipe the caps clean with a soft-bristled mushroom brush or a lightly dampened kitchen or paper towel. Arrange the caps on the grill pan in the smoker. Leaving the lid ajar by 1 inch (2.5 cm), place the pan over medium-high heat until it begins to smoke, then close the lid completely. Cook until the mushrooms are tender, 10–12 minutes. Remove from the smoker and set aside to cool.

3 Alternatively, if you do not have a smoker, soak 4 bamboo skewers in water to cover for about 30 minutes. Prepare a charcoal or gas grill for indirect grilling over medium-high heat. When the grill is ready, drain the skewers and thread the mushrooms on them. Place on the grill rack and grill, turning occasionally, until tender, 3–4 minutes. Set aside to cool.

4 In a large nonreactive bowl, combine the greens, smoked mushrooms, and red onion. Season to taste with salt and pepper.

5 In a small nonreactive saucepan over medium-low heat, warm the dressing, being careful not to let it boil. When the vinaigrette is warm to the touch, pour it over the mixed greens. Using tongs, toss the salad gently. Taste and adjust the seasoning.

6 Arrange the salad on warmed plates and shave the cheese on top using a vegetable peeler.

Serve with a full-bodied white Burgundy to balance the strong flavors of the smoked mushrooms and vinaigrette.

CRISPY QUAIL SALAD WITH ORANGES AND PECAN VINAIGRETTE

Fall colors and flavors are abundant in this recipe from celebrated New Orleans chef Susan Spicer, owner of the landmark Bayona and cocreator of Herbsaint and Cobalt restaurants. Quail, oranges, and pecans all appear on Louisiana's culinary calendar around the same time—and bourbon is always in season. Autumn also brings the sugarcane harvest, along with one of its by-products, cane vinegar. (Steen's, which also bottles cane syrup and molasses, is the best-known brand.) Don't be discouraged by the long list of ingredients. The preparation is actually quite simple, and the results are spectacular.

1 In a large bowl, combine the brown sugar, soy sauce, the 1 tablespoon bourbon, 1 teaspoon of the orange zest, and ½ teaspoon salt. Add the quail, turn to coat, and let stand for 1 hour at room temperature, or cover and refrigerate for at least 4 hours or overnight.

2 To make the dressing for the salad, in a small nonreactive saucepan over medium-high heat, combine the shallots, orange juice, the remaining 1 teaspoon orange zest, and the vinegar and bring to a boil. Reduce the heat to medium-low and simmer until reduced by half, about 10 minutes. Scrape the liquid into a bowl and slowly add the olive oil and pecan oil (if using), whisking constantly until the dressing is thick and creamy. Stir in the remaining 1 teaspoon bourbon and season to taste with salt and pepper. Set aside.

3 To segment the oranges for the salad, cut a slice off the top and bottom of each orange. Stand each orange upright on a cutting board. Following the contour of each orange and rotating it with each cut, slice downward to remove the peel, pith, and membrane. Cut the sections free from the membrane and place in a bowl. Set aside.

4 Preheat the oven to 200°F (95°C). Prepare the tempura batter and set aside. Remove the quail from the marinade and pat dry. Line an ovenproof platter with paper towels.

5 Pour canola oil to a depth of 3 inches (7.5 cm) into a deep, heavy saucepan or a deep fryer and heat to 350°F (180°C) on a deep-frying thermometer. A thermometer is essential to maintain the correct temperature for the lightest results.

6 Using a heavy knife, cut each quail in half lengthwise. Dip a quail half into the tempura batter, allowing the excess to drip off, and then carefully slip it into the hot oil. Fry 2 or 3 quail halves at once, making sure not to crowd the pan. Turn each quail half once, and fry until golden, about 4 minutes total. Using tongs or a wire skimmer, transfer to the paper towel–lined platter and place in the oven to keep warm. Repeat until all the quail are fried.

7 To finish the salad, in a large bowl, combine the lettuces, celery, and red onion and toss to mix. Whisk the dressing briefly, then drizzle just enough of the dressing over the salad to coat lightly and toss again. Divide the salad among individual plates and garnish with the orange segments. Cut each fried quail half in half crosswise, and place 4 quarters on each salad. Drizzle with the remaining dressing. Sprinkle with the pecans and serve at once.

Serve with a dry rosé, such as a Pinot Noir rosé or a rosé from the Loire Valley.

2 tablespoons dark brown sugar

1 teaspoon soy sauce

1 tablespoon bourbon, plus 1 teaspoon

2 teaspoons grated orange zest

Sea salt

4 semi-boneless quail (page 186)

1 tablespoon minced shallots

½ cup (4 fl oz/125 ml) fresh orange juice

2 tablespoons cider vinegar

½ cup (4 fl oz/125 ml) olive oil

2 tablespoons pecan oil (optional)

Freshly ground pepper

2 oranges

Tempura batter (page 187)

Canola oil for deep-frying

4–6 cups (4–6 oz/125–185 g) assorted lettuces

1 cup (4 oz/125 g) thinly sliced celery hearts

¼ red onion, thinly sliced

Toasted spicy-sweet pecans (page 186) for garnish

Makes 4 servings

SALAD OF SATSUMAS, ROASTED BEETS, PECANS, AND FARMER'S CHEESE

Citrus fruits were transplanted from Spain to Louisiana in the eighteenth century by Jesuit priests, who also introduced the fruits to Florida, Texas, and California. Oranges thrive in Plaquemines Parish, just south of New Orleans, but no citrus fruit is more eagerly awaited than the seedless mandarins known as satsumas. These sweet fruits are at their peak during the cool days of autumn, when heavy sacks of them are draped over produce stands, and vendors sell their wares on busy streets. They provide the sparkle in this vibrant salad from New Orleans chef Corbin Evans of Lulu's and its spinoff, Lulu's in the Garden.

4 small beets

FOR THE HONEY VINAIGRETTE
2 tablespoons wildflower honey

2 tablespoons red wine vinegar

2 tablespoons rice wine vinegar

Sea salt and freshly ground pepper

½ cup (4 fl oz/125 ml) extra-virgin olive oil

FOR THE FARMER'S CHEESE
½ cup (4 oz/125 g) cottage cheese

½ cup (4 oz/125 g) cream cheese

½ cup (2½ oz/75 g) fresh goat cheese

Sea salt and freshly ground pepper

6 satsumas or other seedless mandarin oranges, such as clementines

2 heads Bibb lettuce, leaves left whole

½ cup (2 oz/60 g) chopped toasted spicy-sweet pecans (page 186)

Makes 6 servings

1 Preheat the oven to 450°F (230°C). If the beet greens are still attached, cut them off, leaving 1 inch (2.5 cm) of the stem attached to avoid piercing the skin (leave the root attached as well). Save the greens for another use. Scrub the unpeeled beets, wrap in aluminum foil, and roast until easily pierced with the tip of a knife, about 1 hour. Remove from the oven, unwrap, and when cool enough to handle, peel the beets, trim the root, and cut into slices ¼ inch (6 mm) thick. Set aside to cool completely.

2 While the beets are roasting, make the honey vinaigrette. In a nonreactive bowl, whisk together the honey and vinegars. Season to taste with salt and pepper, whisking until dissolved. Slowly add the olive oil in a steady stream, whisking constantly until emulsified. Taste and adjust the seasoning.

3 To make the farmer's cheese, in a food processor, combine the cheeses and blend until smooth. Season to taste with salt and pepper.

4 Cut a slice off the top and bottom of each satsuma. Stand each satsuma upright on a cutting board. Following the contour of each satsuma and rotating it with each cut, slice downward to remove the peel, pith, and membrane. Cut the sections free from the membrane and place in a bowl.

5 Divide the lettuce among individual salad plates. Arrange the satsuma segments and beet slices on top of the lettuce. Drizzle with the vinaigrette. Top each serving with an equal amount of the pecans and a scoop of the farmer's cheese and serve at once.

Serve with an earthy Sangiovese or Rosé d'Anjou to complement the beets and toasted pecans.

OYSTERS EN BROCHETTE

Los Angeles journalist Priscilla Fleming Vayda spent her childhood on the bayous of Lafitte, Louisiana, where she would run straight to the dock on Saturdays to blow her entire twenty-five-cent allowance on "the salty, slippery bliss of raw oysters," downing a cool two dozen fresh off the boats. She passed along this old family recipe, which her mother made with wild raccoon oysters, named for the resourceful creatures that often beat humans to the harvest. This unabashedly retro dish is still served at many Creole restaurants.

1 If using rosemary sprigs, strip off most of the leaves, keeping about 2 inches (5 cm) of leaves at the top. Soak the rosemary branches or bamboo skewers in water to cover for 30 minutes. Preheat the broiler (grill), or prepare a fire in a charcoal grill for direct grilling over high heat.

2 Cut the bacon in half crosswise. In a small frying pan over medium-high heat, fry the bacon until lightly browned but still flexible, about 3 minutes on each side. Drain on paper towels.

3 Place the oysters on a plate, squeeze the lemon evenly over them, and then season the oysters with several grinds of pepper. Wrap each oyster in a half bacon slice, and thread 3 or 4 oysters onto each rosemary sprig or skewer.

4 Place the sprigs or skewers on the grill rack about 5 inches (13 cm) from the fire and grill, turning once, until the bacon is crisp but the oysters are still plump and juicy, 3–4 minutes on each side. Alternatively, arrange on a broiler pan or a rimmed baking sheet, place under the broiler, and broil (grill), turning once, for about the same amount of time.

5 Remove the skewers from the grill or broiler. To serve, divide the bread slices among individual plates and slide the oysters off the skewers onto the bread. Serve at once.

Serve with a dry white wine, such as a Chablis or Fumé Blanc to enhance the salty oysters and smoky bacon.

**4 sturdy rosemary branches or
4 bamboo skewers, each
12 inches (30 cm) long**

6–8 thin slices best-quality bacon

12–16 oysters, shucked

¼ lemon

**Freshly ground white or
black pepper**

**8 thin slices French bread,
toasted and buttered, or 8 buttered
toast points**

Makes 4 servings

Oyster Bed to Oyster Bar

Prehistoric shell mounds found in southern Louisiana are proof that Native Americans feasted on oysters for thousands of years before they were harvested by early French settlers. However, serious oyster cultivation in Louisiana began with the arrival of Slavonian fishermen in the mid-1840s. Working in the estuary waters south of New Orleans, the Slavonians developed the modern system of cultivation, transferring oysters from overcrowded reefs to more favorable beds with good salinity and a steady current. Oystermen have leased these water bottoms from the state since 1902. Now thousands of leases, spread over great stretches of coastal land, are operated along the Louisiana shoreline.

Today's oysterman travels aboard a motorized boat towing a dredge that scoops "seed oysters" from public grounds. He hauls them back to his lease, then washes them overboard. They are left to grow for one to two years, then dredged onto the lugger, where they're cleaned for the market, and bound for raw bars, cast-iron frying pans, soup pots, and grills.

SOUPS AND GUMBOS

Big soup pots get plenty of use in New Orleans, where every cook swears

by his own version of gumbo, whether it showcases seafood or wild game.

In New Orleans, soup can be a prelude to the main course, or the main course itself. It is an excellent vehicle for leftovers, transforming Sunday's ham into Monday's bean soup, or the remains of a roasted chicken into a fragrant and filling gumbo. Even in the finest restaurants, Louisiana soups, from a spicy Creole turtle soup to a creamy bisque of oysters and artichokes, tend to be rich and hearty. Gumbo, however, remains the state's signature dish, and like Louisiana it is at once homey and exotic, earthy and elegant. Ask a dozen cooks how to make it and you'll get a dozen different recipes.

SEAFOOD GUMBO

Gumbo is the name given to a wide array of rich soups served throughout the coastal South. Some are thickened with okra, some are thickened with a roux, a cooked mixture of fat and flour, and others by the addition of filé (sassafras) powder. This version uses a combination of both okra and roux. In New Orleans and bayou country, the stockpot is generally filled with shellfish, while the prairie Cajuns prefer a hearty mix of chicken and smoked sausage. Both types of gumbo, however, are always served over steamed rice, along with plenty of hot French bread or corn bread.

1 To make the stock, peel and devein the shrimp and remove the heads. Place the shrimp in an airtight container and refrigerate until ready to use. Rinse the heads and shells in a colander, then place in a stockpot. Quarter the onion and garlic lengthwise, cut the celery in half, and add to the stockpot along with 8 cups (64 fl oz/2 l) water. Bring to a boil over high heat, reduce the heat to low, and simmer, uncovered, for 2 hours. Strain through a fine-mesh sieve, discarding the solids. Return the stock to the pot, adding water if necessary to make 6 cups (48 fl oz/ 1.5 l), and set aside.

2 To make the gumbo, chop the yellow onions and celery. Seed, trim, and chop the bell pepper. Set aside. Peel and seed the tomatoes (page 187), then chop. You should have about 3 cups (18 oz/560 g) chopped tomatoes. Set aside. Trim the okra and cut crosswise into ½-inch (12-mm) slices. Set aside.

3 Heat a large, heavy frying pan, preferably cast iron, over medium-high heat just until it begins to smoke. Add the oil and then carefully whisk in the flour and continue whisking until you have a dark brown roux, 3–5 minutes. Add the chopped yellow onions, celery, and bell pepper and cook, stirring constantly, until the vegetables are tender and lightly browned, about 3 minutes. Add the minced garlic and cook, stirring, for about 2 minutes longer.

4 Bring the reserved stock to a boil over medium-high heat. Add the vegetable-roux mixture to the stock by large spoonfuls, stirring each addition until incorporated before adding more. Add the tomatoes, okra, thyme, cayenne to taste, and bay leaves, season to taste with salt and black pepper, and return to a boil. Reduce the heat to medium-low and cook for 30 minutes longer, skimming occasionally to remove the excess oil.

5 Add the reserved shrimp, reduce the heat to medium-low, and simmer just until they turn pink, about 2 minutes. Stir in the green onions, crabmeat, and oysters and simmer just until the edges of the oysters curl, 2–3 minutes. Taste and adjust the seasoning with salt and black pepper or cayenne.

6 Remove the bay leaves and discard. Spoon the rice into warmed bowls and ladle the gumbo over the top. Serve at once.

Serve with a crisp white wine such as an unoaked French Chardonnay.

FOR THE STOCK

2 lb (1 kg) shrimp (prawns), with heads attached

1 *each* yellow onion, garlic clove, and celery stalk with leaves

FOR THE GUMBO

2 yellow onions, peeled

2 celery stalks, trimmed

1 green bell pepper (capsicum)

3 lb (1.5 kg) tomatoes

1 lb (500 g) okra

½ cup (4 fl oz/125 ml) corn oil

½ cup (2½ oz/75 g) all-purpose (plain) flour

5 cloves garlic, finely minced

½ teaspoon dried thyme

Cayenne pepper

3 bay leaves

Sea salt and black pepper

6 green (spring) onions, including tender green parts, chopped

1 lb (500 g) lump crabmeat

12 oysters, shucked, with their liquor

Steamed white rice for serving

Makes 8–12 servings

RED BEAN AND ANDOUILLE SOUP

Creamy red beans are favored in New Orleans, but this hearty meal in a bowl would still be delicious made from black beans, Great Northerns, black-eyed peas, pintos, or a blend. You might also stop before puréeing the beans, adding the reserved ham at that point, for the traditional red beans served over steamed rice. It's also fine to substitute chicken or vegetable stock for the stock made with the ham bone, to replace the andouille with another lean smoked sausage, or to forgo the meat altogether to create a vegetarian dish. Serve the soup with a side of corn bread and a bottle of hot sauce.

1 lb (500 g) dried red kidney beans

1 meaty ham bone, about 1 lb (500 g), trimmed of fat

1 yellow onion, chopped

1 celery stalk, chopped

2 cloves garlic, chopped

1 large bay leaf

½ teaspoon dried thyme

1 teaspoon Tabasco, or to taste

Sea salt and freshly ground pepper

½ lb (250 g) andouille or other lean smoked sausage, cut into slices ¼ inch (6 mm) thick

Chopped green (spring) onions, including tender green parts, for garnish

Makes 6–8 servings

1 Pick over the beans and discard any misshapen beans or stones. Rinse the beans and drain. Place in a large bowl, add plenty of cold water to cover, and let soak overnight.

2 In a large soup pot over high heat, combine the ham bone and 6 cups (48 fl oz/1.5 l) water and bring to a boil. Reduce the heat to medium-low and cook at a lively simmer for 1 hour, skimming frequently to remove any foam that rises to the surface.

3 Remove the pot from the heat. Using tongs, carefully lift the ham bone out of the pot and set aside on a plate. When cool enough to handle, remove the meat from the bone, discarding any fat. Set the meat aside. Using a large spoon, skim off any fat from the surface of the stock. Return the bone to the stock.

4 Drain the beans and add to the stock along with the yellow onion, celery, garlic, bay leaf, and thyme. Place the pot over high heat and bring to a boil. Reduce the heat to low, cover, and simmer, stirring frequently to prevent sticking, until the beans are tender, about 2 hours.

5 Remove and discard the ham bone and bay leaf and let the soup cool slightly. Scoop out 3 cups (21 oz/655 g) of the beans with a little liquid and place in a food processor or blender. Process until smooth, then return the purée to the pot. Cut the reserved ham into bite-sized pieces and add to the pot. Season to taste with the Tabasco, salt, and pepper.

6 In a large frying pan over medium-high heat, brown the andouille slices on both sides, about 2 minutes per side. Remove from the heat.

7 Ladle the soup into warmed bowls, and top each serving with several slices of andouille and a sprinkle of green onions. Serve at once.

Serve with a hearty red or amber ale.

SWEET POTATO VICHYSSOISE

Although many people assume vichyssoise is a French dish, it is actually American, with strong Gallic roots. Created in New York during the early twentieth century by chef Louis Diat, it is simply a chilled, cream-enriched version of the humble leek and potato soup he remembered from his childhood home near Vichy, France. Here, it gets a flash of New World color and flavor from Louisiana sweet potatoes and is energized by fresh ginger and cayenne. At once cool and spicy, it is a fine starter for a holiday meal or autumn picnic.

1 In a saucepan over medium-high heat, combine the stock, sweet potatoes, and leeks and bring to a boil. Reduce the heat to medium-low, cover, and simmer until the potatoes are tender but not mushy, about 20 minutes.

2 Remove from the heat and let cool slightly. Working in batches if necessary, combine the sweet potato mixture, ½ teaspoon white pepper, the ginger, and the cayenne in a food processor or blender and process until a smooth purée forms. Pour into a large bowl and let cool to lukewarm. Stir in the cream and season to taste with salt. Cover and refrigerate until well chilled, at least 4 hours or up to 2 days. (The flavor improves with time.)

3 Taste and adjust the seasoning. Ladle the soup into chilled bowls and garnish with the chives. Serve at once.

Serve with a light, floral, and aromatic white wine such as Viognier.

4 cups (32 fl oz/1 l) chicken stock

2 or 3 sweet potatoes, 1½ lb (750 g) total weight, peeled and quartered

2 small leeks, white and tender green parts only, chopped

Freshly ground white pepper

2 teaspoons peeled and grated fresh ginger

¼ teaspoon cayenne pepper

½ cup (4 fl oz/125 ml) heavy (double) cream

Sea salt

Chopped fresh chives for garnish

Makes 6 servings

Sweet on Yams

Louisiana yams suffer from a bit of an identity crisis. First, they're not actually yams, which are starchier, contain less sugar, and are native to tropical and subtropical regions. They also differ from sweet potatoes grown in the northern United States, which are pale-fleshed, firm, and mealy.

Southerners prefer the moist texture and extrasweet flavor of these bright orange beauties, which were originally imported from Puerto Rico. Their name was probably shortened from the Senegalese *nyami,* so-called because they reminded African slaves of similar starchy tubers from their homeland. Cultivation was encouraged in the eighteenth and nineteenth centuries, when both Louis XV and Empress Josephine were great consumers of the vegetable.

In Louisiana, yams are not just for Thanksgiving. Oven baking—about 1 hour at 350°F (180°C)—is best for maximum flavor. Don't wrap them in foil, which will just steam away the juices that should brown into syrupy caramel drips. They are also great sliced, skewered, and grilled over medium-hot coals until tender.

CRAWFISH BISQUE

Unlike the creamy bisques of France, this old Louisiana delicacy is spicy and substantial, usually served as a meal in one bowl (or two, or three). Traditionally it's brimming with meaty crawfish tails and their cleaned shells, the latter painstakingly filled with deviled crawfish. This process begins with a twenty-five-pound (twelve-kilogram) sack of live mudbugs, followed by a lot of mess, bother, and disgruntled aunts huddled around a kitchen table shoving stuffing into dozens of tiny shells. Their children are more likely to make this simplified version, afloat with little balls of stuffing, known as boulettes.

6 cups (48 fl oz/1.5 l) fish stock
or chicken stock or water

1 green bell pepper (capsicum)

½ cup (4 fl oz/125 ml) corn oil

½ cup (2½ oz/75 g) all-purpose
(plain) flour

2 yellow onions, finely chopped

3 celery stalks, finely chopped

3 cloves garlic, minced

2 cups (16 fl oz/500 ml) fresh
tomato purée (page 187)

¼ teaspoon cayenne pepper

2 large bay leaves

4 teaspoons fresh thyme leaves

Sea salt and black pepper

¼ cup (2 oz/60 g) unsalted butter

2 lb (1 kg) cooked crawfish tails

⅔ cup (2 oz/60 g) green (spring)
onions, finely chopped

4 tablespoons (⅓ oz/10 g) minced
fresh flat-leaf (Italian) parsley

1 teaspoon Tabasco

1½ cups (3 oz/90 g) fresh
bread crumbs

Juice of ½ lemon, strained

2 large eggs, lightly beaten

Makes 6–8 servings

1 In a saucepan over high heat, bring the stock to a boil. Seed and finely chop the bell pepper.

2 In a heavy soup pot over medium-high heat, warm the oil just until it begins to smoke. Whisk in the flour and continue whisking until you have a medium brown roux, 3–4 minutes. Add 1 chopped yellow onion, 2 chopped celery stalks, and the bell pepper and cook, stirring constantly, until tender and lightly browned. Add the garlic and stir just until it releases its fragrance, about 1 minute. Add the tomato purée and stir for 2–3 minutes longer. Add the boiling stock, cayenne, bay leaves, and 2 teaspoons of the thyme, and season with salt and black pepper. Return the soup to a boil, reduce the heat to maintain a lively simmer, and cook uncovered, stirring occasionally and scraping the bottom to prevent sticking, until the bisque is the consistency of heavy (double) cream, about 1 hour.

3 Meanwhile, prepare the boulettes. Preheat the oven to 375°F (190°C). Butter a heavy, rimmed baking sheet. In a large frying pan over medium heat, melt the butter. Add the remaining chopped yellow onion and celery, and cook until golden, 7–8 minutes. Peel and coarsely chop 1 lb (500 g) of the crawfish tails and add to the onion mixture with ⅓ cup (1 oz/30 g) green onions, 2 tablespoons of the parsley,

the remaining 2 teaspoons thyme, the Tabasco, and the bread crumbs. Stir, remove from the heat, add the lemon juice, and season to taste with salt and black pepper. Stir in the eggs until the ingredients are well combined. Using wet hands so that the mixture doesn't stick, form into approximately 24 small ovals and arrange on the prepared baking sheet. Bake the boulettes until they are puffed and well browned, 20–30 minutes.

4 When the bisque is ready, peel the remaining 1 lb (500 g) crawfish tails and add to the bisque. Carefully add the boulettes. Simmer, gently stirring occasionally, for about 20 minutes.

5 Taste and adjust the seasoning. Then stir in the remaining ⅓ cup (1 oz/30 g) green onions and remaining 2 tablespoons parsley. Ladle into warmed bowls and serve at once.

Serve with a full-bodied lager.

Note: Fresh or frozen crawfish and crawfish tail meat can be purchased from a number of sources; see Ingredient Sources on page 187.

OYSTER STEW

Some people like their oysters en brochette *(on skewers), others prefer them roasted or fried, but soup is the ideal medium for coddling these sensitive creatures that can overcook in the blink of an eye. Plopped into simmering liquid at the last moment, they poach into plump delicacies that still taste of salt and sea. Creamy oyster stew is a Southern classic that is served throughout Louisiana, especially as a first course for holiday dinners. It frequently appears on humbler tables, too, since it's so easy to prepare.*

1 In a small saucepan over medium heat, warm the milk until small bubbles appear around the edge of the pan. Reduce the heat to the lowest setting.

2 In a separate saucepan over medium heat, melt the butter. Add the green onions and sauté until soft but not browned, 1–2 minutes. Add the oysters with their liquor, parsley, and celery salt and simmer just until the edges of the oysters curl, 2–3 minutes.

3 Add the hot milk, stir to blend, and simmer for 1 minute longer. Do not allow the soup to boil, or it will curdle. Season to taste with salt and white pepper.

4 Ladle the soup into warmed bowls, garnish with oyster crackers, and serve at once.

Serve with a slightly acidic and fruity white wine such as Muscadet or Pinot Grigio.

3 cups (24 fl oz/750 ml) whole milk or half-and-half (half cream)

3 tablespoons unsalted butter

¼ cup (¾ oz/20 g) thinly sliced green (spring) onions, including tender green parts

24 oysters, shucked, with their liquor (page 53)

1 tablespoon minced fresh flat-leaf (Italian) parsley

½ teaspoon celery salt

Sea salt and freshly ground white pepper

Oyster crackers for garnish

Makes 4 servings

Reviving the Réveillon

Christmas Eve in nineteenth-century Louisiana was a night for camaraderie. In New Orleans, families visited from house to house on the way to midnight mass at the Saint Louis Cathedral, while country people walked to church along Mississippi River levees alight with bonfires.

After services, most would return home for a toast to the holiday and a late-night breakfast. In grand city houses the meal was known as the Réveillon, a feast that traditionally included selections of fish, fowl, and flesh. Tables would be spread with delicacies such as *daube glacé* (beef layered with vegetables in aspic), oyster stew, sweetbreads, elaborate egg dishes, pastries, and crystallized fruits. The night ended with eggnog and a jelly-filled cake dripping with wine or rum and topped with whipped cream.

Today the spirit of the Réveillon tradition continues at many of the city's finest restaurants, which offer special menus from December 1 through 25. The lavish four- or five-course meals provide diners a (relatively) inexpensive opportunity to experience the best of classic and contemporary local cuisine.

DUCK AND WILD MUSHROOM GUMBO

In addition to okra and roux, filé, a khaki green powder of ground sassafras leaves, can be used as a seasoning and thickener for gumbo. Because filé becomes stringy if it is boiled, it's best added during the final stage of simmering, as in this recipe. This dark and smoky gumbo was adapted from a recipe created by Matthew Murphy, chef at the Ritz-Carlton, New Orleans. Despite its tony pedigree, it has solid roots in Cajun country, where wild mushrooms flourish and duck hunting is a popular sport. In New Orleans and the southern coastal areas, gumbo commonly includes seafood, rather than fowl or wild game.

FOR THE ROASTED DUCK AND STOCK

1 duck, about 6 lb (3 kg), preferably a Muscovy

4 celery stalks with leaves

2 *each* cloves garlic, yellow onions, and carrots, unpeeled

2 *each* thyme sprigs and bay leaves

FOR THE GUMBO

2 *each* yellow onions and green bell peppers (capsicums)

½ cup (4 fl oz/125 ml) corn oil

½ cup (2½ oz/75 g) all-purpose (plain) flour

3 cloves garlic, finely minced

¼–½ teaspoon cayenne pepper

Freshly ground white pepper

1 teaspoon fresh thyme leaves

2 bay leaves

1 lb (500 g) andouille sausage

½ lb (250 g) fresh wild mushrooms

Sea salt

2 tablespoons filé, plus more for garnish

Steamed white rice for serving

Chopped green (spring) onions

Makes 6 servings

1 To prepare the roasted duck and stock, preheat the oven to 350°F (180°C). Using a fork, lightly prick the skin all over the duck, being careful not to pierce the flesh. Place the duck, breast side down, on a rack in a roasting pan. Roast until the skin is browned and an instant-read thermometer inserted into the thigh registers 180°F (82°C), 1½–2 hours.

2 Remove the duck from the oven and, when cool enough to handle, remove the skin and discard. Remove the meat from the bones and place it in an airtight container in the refrigerator until needed. Place the bones in a stockpot. Coarsely chop the celery, quarter the garlic cloves and onions lengthwise, and quarter the carrots crosswise. Add the vegetables to the pot along with the thyme, bay leaves, and 4 qt (4 l) water. Bring to a boil over high heat, reduce the heat to maintain a lively simmer, and cook, uncovered, for 5–6 hours. Strain through a fine-mesh sieve, discarding the solids. You should have about 2½ qt (2.5 l) stock. Return the stock to the pot, adding water if necessary to make 2½ qt (2.5 l), and set aside.

3 To make the gumbo, chop the yellow onions and seed and chop the bell peppers and set aside. Heat a large, heavy frying pan, preferably cast iron, over medium-high heat just until it begins to smoke. Add the oil and then whisk in the flour and continue whisking until you have a dark brown roux, about 4 minutes. Add the chopped yellow onions and bell peppers and cook, stirring constantly, until tender and browned, about 3 minutes. Add the garlic and cook, stirring, for about 2 minutes longer.

4 Bring the reserved stock to a boil over medium-high heat. Add the roux mixture to the stock by spoonfuls, stirring each addition until incorporated before adding more. Add the cayenne to taste, ¼ teaspoon white pepper, the thyme, and the bay leaves, and boil for 10 minutes.

5 Meanwhile, cut the andouille into slices ½ inch (12 mm) thick. Wipe the mushrooms clean and slice thickly. In a large frying pan over medium-high heat, cook the sausage slices, turning once, until browned, about 2 minutes per side, then add to the gumbo. Add the mushrooms to the frying pan and sauté for 1 minute, then add to the gumbo. Reduce the heat to a low boil and cook the gumbo for about 30 minutes to blend the flavors.

6 Shred the duck meat into bite-sized pieces, add to the gumbo, and simmer for 15 minutes longer to heat the duck meat and blend the flavors. Season generously with salt and white pepper. Using a large spoon, skim off any fat from the surface. Stir in the 2 tablespoons filé and simmer gently for 1–2 minutes; do not allow the gumbo to boil.

7 Remove the bay leaves and discard, then taste and adjust the seasoning. Spoon the rice into warmed bowls and ladle the gumbo over the top. Sprinkle lightly with filé and green onions. Serve at once.

Serve with a young, dry red wine such as Pinot Noir.

MOCK TURTLE SOUP

Resourceful Creole cooks probably created this highly seasoned chowder to disguise the rather swampy taste of turtle meat, so here we use veal instead. It's an open secret that many chefs do the same. Besides, fresh cleaned turtles are hard to come by, especially outside Louisiana. Quite different from the clear consommés of Europe and the American East Coast, the New Orleans soup, typically served on special occasions, is wonderfully complex and chunky, enlivened by herbs, spices, and fresh lemon.

1 In a heavy soup pot over medium-high heat, warm the oil. Add the veal and cook, stirring frequently, until browned on all sides, 5–8 minutes. Add the yellow onion, celery, bay leaves, thyme, paprika, and cayenne to taste and cook, stirring frequently, until the vegetables are tender and lightly browned, about 9 minutes. Add the flour and cook for 5 minutes, stirring constantly. Add the garlic, tomato purée, stock, Worcestershire sauce, and fish sauce (if using). Season well with salt and black pepper. Return the soup to a boil, reduce the heat to low, and simmer uncovered, stirring occasionally, for 1 hour to blend the flavors.

2 While the soup is simmering, remove the seeds from the lemon half, then chop coarsely. In a mini food processor, process the lemon until finely ground. Peel the eggs and chop finely.

3 After the soup has simmered for 1 hour, add the lemon, eggs, parsley, and green onions, stir well, and simmer for 30 minutes longer.

4 Remove the bay leaves and discard. Stir in the sherry, then taste and adjust the seasoning. Ladle into warmed bowls and serve at once.

Serve with a medium-dry Amontillado sherry.

⅓ cup (3 fl oz/80 ml) canola oil

2 lb (1 kg) boneless veal shoulder, finely chopped

1 yellow onion, finely chopped

2 celery stalks, finely chopped

3 bay leaves

2 teaspoons minced fresh thyme

1 teaspoon paprika

½–1 teaspoon cayenne pepper

⅓ cup (2 oz/60 g) all-purpose (plain) flour

2 cloves garlic, minced

2 cups (16 fl oz/500 ml) fresh tomato purée (page 187)

6 cups (48 fl oz/1.5 l) beef stock

1 tablespoon Worcestershire sauce

2 tablespoons Thai fish sauce (optional)

Sea salt and black pepper

½ small lemon

4 hard-boiled eggs

½ cup (¾ oz/20 g) minced fresh flat-leaf (Italian) parsley

½ cup (1 oz/45 g) chopped tender green (spring) onion tops

½ cup (4 fl oz/125 ml) dry sherry

Makes 10–12 servings

Swamp Things

People in Louisiana like to boast that they'll eat anything that doesn't eat them first—pretty bold talk for residents of a swamp. In addition to crawfish, many other cold-blooded ingredients emerge from the primordial ooze.

No reptile was harmed in the making of this mock turtle soup, but in Louisiana, turtles are now cultivated by aqua-culturists, who supply chefs and home cooks with the dark, lean meat. Beyond the Gulf Coast, place a special order with a local seafood market or check with Chinese or Latin grocers.

Alligators have long been valued for their hides, a popularity that put them on the brink of extinction by the 1960s. They were saved by a hunting ban, which was lifted in the early 1980s, when the Cajun cooking fad made the firm white meat so trendy that people began farming the critters. Traditionally the meat is stewed in a spicy tomato-based sauce, or else fried or ground into sausages.

Frogs are prized in all French kitchens, but only for their legs, which are usually battered and fried. The tender white meat tastes like chicken.

GUMBO Z'HERBES

This gumbo is made with greens, which are called z'herbes in the Creole dialect, from the French des herbes, explains regional historian Carolyn Kolb, who contributed this recipe. Because it can be made without meat, the fragrant stew is a traditional Lenten dish in New Orleans, especially on Good Friday, when the mix of greens is supposed to represent the twelve apostles. Even so, many cooks risk damnation by simmering a ham bone with the stock or adding chopped smoked sausage to the roux. Serve with Iron-Skillet Corn Bread with Hot-Pepper Jelly (page 158).

FOR THE VEGETABLE STOCK

5 carrots

2 yellow onions

3 celery stalks

Bouquet garni of 1 sprig *each* fresh flat-leaf (Italian) parsley and thyme and 1 bay leaf

FOR THE GUMBO

5 tablespoons (3 fl oz/80 ml) canola or corn oil

¼ cup (1½ oz/45 g) all-purpose (plain) flour

3 yellow onions, chopped

1 celery stalk, chopped

1 green bell pepper (capsicum), seeded and chopped

2 cloves garlic, minced

20 okra pods, sliced into thin rounds (optional)

Sea salt and freshly ground black pepper

Cayenne pepper

About 3 lb (1.5 kg) assorted greens such as collard, dandelion mustard, spinach, and/or escarole

Steamed white rice for serving

Makes 6–8 servings

1 To make the vegetable stock, preheat the oven to 350°F (180°C). Peel and coarsely chop the carrots, quarter the onions lengthwise, and cut the celery stalks into 3–4 pieces each. Spead the vegetables on a lightly oiled rimmed baking sheet. Place in the oven and roast, stirring occasionally, until browned, about 25 minutes.

2 Place the parsley and thyme sprigs and bay leaf for the bouquet garni on a square of cheesecloth (muslin), bring the corners together, and tie securely with kitchen string.

3 In a stockpot, combine the roasted vegetables, bouquet garni, and 3 qt (3 l) cold water. Bring to a boil over high heat, then reduce the heat to low and simmer, uncovered, until the stock is reduced to 6 cups (48 fl oz/1.5 l), 3–4 hours. Strain through a fine-mesh sieve, discarding the solids. Return the stock to the pot and place over low heat to keep warm.

4 To make the gumbo, in a heavy, nonreactive soup pot over medium-high heat, warm the oil. Whisk in the flour and continue whisking until you have a dark brown roux, 3–5 minutes. Immediately add the onions,

celery, bell pepper, garlic, and okra (if using). Stir until the vegetables are tender and the onions are translucent, 5–6 minutes. Ladle in the stock, stirring each addition until incorporated before adding more. Season to taste with salt, black pepper, and cayenne. Bring to a boil, then reduce the heat to low, cover, and simmer for 30 minutes.

5 Rinse the greens well, trim off any tough stems, and chop coarsely. Add to the pot, stir well, cover, and continue to simmer until the greens are tender, at least 15 minutes. If you have used okra, the seeds will be dispersed throughout the gumbo when it is done.

6 If the gumbo seems too thick, add water as needed to thin to the desired consistency. Taste and adjust the seasoning. Spoon steamed rice into warmed bowls and ladle the gumbo over the top. Serve at once.

As this is a Lenten dish, a nonalcoholic iced tea would be appropriate. Garnish the glasses with fresh mint sprigs to add another good-luck green to the table.

MAIN COURSES

Fresh regional seafood will always anchor menus in Creole and Cajun

restaurants, but wild game and sausages are mainstays on many tables.

Grand old Creole restaurants continue the tradition of serving the dishes—seafood with butter sauces, beef with béarnaise—that have made New Orleans a culinary capital. Yet even in the birthplace of deep-fried turkey, a lighter side is emerging. Open kitchens give diners a view of wood-fired grills, and citrus vinaigrettes and fresh relishes sometimes replace rich sauces. Home cooks have also become more health conscious, though slow-pot stews and étouffées are still colored by a rich brown roux, sausage remains the seasoning of choice, and special occasions still call for sweet glazed ham.

NEW ORLEANS–STYLE BARBECUED SHRIMP

The shrimp in this dish are neither grilled over an open fire nor smothered in barbecue sauce, yet the name has persisted for generations. Jumbo shrimp are slowly simmered in a scandalous amount of butter, then spiked with plenty of herbs and spices. Traditionally they are served unpeeled in wide soup bowls, accompanied by lots of napkins and French bread for sopping up the sauce. This recipe is from educator and gifted cook Kathy Boyd, a lifelong Louisiana resident, who replaces some of the butter with olive oil for a lighter dish.

1 Preheat the oven to 350°F (180°C). In a large frying pan over medium heat, melt the butter with the olive oil. Add the onion, rosemary, and oregano and cook until the onion is translucent but not browned, about 8 minutes. Add the garlic and cook until the garlic is softened, about 2 minutes longer. Stir in the parsley and remove from the heat. Season well with salt, black pepper, and cayenne.

2 Rinse the shrimp and arrange them in a shallow 4-qt (4-l) baking dish. Pour the warm sauce evenly over the top. Bake uncovered, stirring every 10 minutes, until the shrimp are opaque throughout and the flavors have melded, about 30 minutes.

3 Divide the shrimp and sauce among warmed shallow bowls. Serve at once. Pass the French bread at the table.

Served with a light lager or a dry and spicy white wine, such as an Oregon Pinot Gris.

½ cup (4 oz/125 g) unsalted butter

½ cup (4 fl oz/125 ml) olive oil

1 yellow onion, finely chopped

2 tablespoons dried rosemary

1 tablespoon dried oregano

1 large clove garlic, minced

½ cup (¾ oz/20 g) minced fresh flat-leaf (Italian) parsley

Sea salt and freshly ground black pepper

Cayenne pepper

2 lb (1 kg) extra-large shrimp (prawns), with heads attached

Warmed French bread for serving

Makes 4–6 servings

The Blessing of the Fleet

Along the fringes of coastal Louisiana, narrow roads are lined on one side with boat docks and on the other with shuttered houses perched atop tall pilings, their yards laced with drying nets and crab traps. It is not unusual to drive through water lapping against the roadside, even when no hurricanes threaten, a reminder of the tenuous existence of the families who bring in the catch of the day.

They also brought to these shores a colorful custom that was practiced by their ancestors in Spain, France, and Italy. An annual blessing of the fleet, scheduled at different times in various fishing communities, usually occurs during the white-shrimp (prawn) season in August. A colorful parade of working boats, scrubbed clean and gaily decorated, chugs past a parish priest stationed on land who blesses each boat as it passes. Most are filled to the gunwales with friends, family, food, and drink, all bound for a raucous party on the water. It is a lighthearted celebration, but also a serious ritual for those who spend much of their lives facing the dangers of the Gulf.

STEAK WITH TASSO MARCHAND DE VIN AND TRUFFLED MASHED POTATOES

Ask one hundred New Orleanians to name the city's best restaurants and you would get one hundred different lists, but Commander's Palace would appear on most of them. The Garden District landmark has been the proving ground for some of the country's most famous chefs, including Paul Prudhomme and Emeril Lagasse, and it is known as a trendsetter for contemporary Creole cuisine. Here, a classic meat-and-potatoes meal is updated with tasso (page 44), caramelized onions, and a swirl of truffle oil. Chef Tory McPhail cooks the mushrooms in a stove-top smoker, but this version omits that step.

4 cups (32 fl oz/1 l) veal stock

2 large yellow onions

½ lb (250 g) fresh white mushrooms

¼ cup (2 fl oz/60 ml) canola oil

Sea salt and white pepper

2 lb (1 kg) Yukon gold potatoes

½ cup (4 fl oz/125 ml) buttermilk

½ cup (4 oz/125 g) sour cream

¼ cup (2 oz/60 g) unsalted butter

2 tablespoons truffle oil

FOR THE MARCHAND DE VIN

1 tablespoon unsalted butter

2 tablespoons *each* finely diced shallots and fresh mushrooms

2 tablespoons finely diced tasso

1 tablespoon tomato paste

½ cup (4 fl oz/125 ml) red wine

½ cup (1½ oz/45 g) finely chopped green (spring) onions

4 filet mignon steaks, each about 1½ inches (4 cm) thick

Corn oil

Black pepper and cayenne pepper

Makes 4 servings

1 In a saucepan over medium-high heat, bring the veal stock to a boil and cook until reduced to 2 cups (16 fl oz/ 500 ml), about 5 minutes. Set aside.

2 Thinly slice the onions. Wipe the mushrooms clean, then thinly slice. In a large sauté pan over medium heat, warm the oil. Add the onions and mushrooms and sauté, stirring frequently, until the onions are tender and browned and the mushrooms are cooked through, about 15 minutes. Season to taste with salt and white pepper, cover, and keep warm over low heat.

3 Peel the potatoes. In a large saucepan over high heat, combine the potatoes with water to cover. Bring to a boil, adjust the heat to maintain a steady simmer, and cook until tender when pierced with a fork, 15–20 minutes. Just before the potatoes are ready, in a small saucepan, heat the buttermilk just until small bubbles appear around the edge of the pan; remove from the heat and keep warm.

4 Drain the potatoes and pass them through a potato ricer held over the saucepan, or return them to the saucepan and mash until smooth with a potato masher. Add the hot buttermilk, sour cream, butter, and truffle oil and stir to mix well. Season to taste with salt and white pepper, cover, and keep warm over low heat.

5 To make the marchand de vin, in a large sauté pan over medium heat, melt the butter. Add the shallots, mushrooms, and tasso and cook, stirring frequently, until the shallots have softened, about 3 minutes. Add the tomato paste and cook, stirring, for 3 minutes longer. Pour in the wine and deglaze the pan, stirring with a wooden spoon to dislodge any browned bits from the pan bottom. Continue cooking until the liquid is reduced by half, about 5 minutes. Pour in the reduced veal stock and heat briefly to blend the flavors. Just before serving, add the green onions and season to taste with salt and white pepper.

6 To cook the steaks, coat them evenly with corn oil and season with salt, black pepper, and cayenne. Preheat a large stove-top grill pan over medium-high heat. Place the steaks on the pan and cook, turning once, for 4–5 minutes on each side for rare, 6–7 minutes on each side for medium, or until done to your liking.

7 To serve, spoon the mashed potatoes into the center of warmed individual plates. Place a steak on top of the potatoes and spoon the onions and mushrooms on top. Drizzle the sauce around the perimeter of each plate and serve at once.

Serve with a full-bodied California Cabernet Sauvignon.

LOUISIANA SEAFOOD BOIL

A great backyard party, a real Louisiana seafood boil requires a 50-gallon (190-l) pot on top of a propane burner. This stove-top version turns out a smaller feast, but the flavors are the same. Once you've mastered the basics, as described below, it's time to release your inner Emeril. Exuberant cooks throw extra goodies into the pot to soak up the spicy brew (try sausage links, whole artichokes, or mushrooms). Spread out some newspapers and the table is set. Saltines and cocktail sauce are optional. Cold beer is essential.

1 Pour 8 qt (8 l) water into a large stockpot. Add the oil, onions, celery, lemons, garlic, bay leaves, ginger, crab boil spice mix, salt, cayenne, and peppercorns and bring to a boil over high heat. Boil for 10 minutes.

2 Add the potatoes and boil for 5 minutes. Add the crabs and continue boiling for 15 minutes. Add the corn and boil for 5 minutes longer.

3 Add the shrimp and boil for 1 minute. Turn off the heat and allow the mixture to rest for 5 minutes.

4 Using tongs or a skimmer, retrieve the seafood and vegetables from the pot and serve them warm atop several thicknesses of newspaper or large sheets of parchment (baking) paper, or transfer to a large serving platter. The seafood can also be served at room temperature or chilled. Use a nutcracker or table knife to crack the shells.

Fill a washtub with ice and stock it generously with longneck bottles of Dixie beer, American pilsner, or light lager.

⅓ cup (3 fl oz/80 ml) canola oil

6 yellow onions, unpeeled

4 celery stalks, halved crosswise

2 lemons, unpeeled and quartered

12 cloves garlic

5 bay leaves

2-inch (5-cm) piece fresh ginger, thickly sliced

Crab boil spice mix *(right)* or 6 oz (185 g) packaged whole-spice crab boil

½–¾ cup (4–6 oz/125–185 g) sea salt, or to taste

1 tablespoon cayenne pepper, or to taste

1 tablespoon black peppercorns, or to taste

2–3 lb (1–1.5 kg) small red-skinned potatoes, unpeeled

24 live blue crabs (page 54) or 4–6 small live Dungeness crabs

6 ears corn, husked and halved crosswise

5 lb (2.5 kg) large shrimp (prawns), with heads attached

Makes 8–12 servings

Crab Boil Spice Mix

Nothing attracts friendly neighbors like the scent of a backyard seafood boil, a peppery brew guaranteed to make your mouth (and eyes) water. Much of the flavor comes from a product known locally as crab boil, although the aromatic blend of seasonings is also used for shrimp (prawns) and crawfish. If you can't find one of the commercial dry mixes such as Zatarain's or Rex at your grocery store, the recipe that follows is a good substitute. Both brands also package instant powdered or liquid versions, a convenient way to add a quick splash of briny heat to red beans, seafood salads, or Bloody Marys.

To make your own crab boil, in a bowl, mix together 12 whole cloves, ¼ cup (1 oz/30 g) *each* coriander seeds and mustard seeds, 3 tablespoons dill seeds, 1 tablespoon *each* celery seeds and red pepper flakes, 2 tablespoons whole allspice, 2 teaspoons black peppercorns, and 6 bay leaves, crumbled. Place the mixture on a double-thick square of cheesecloth (muslin), gather the corners together, and tie securely with kitchen string. Makes enough to season 5 lb (2.5 kg) shrimp or 12 blue crabs.

TROUT MEUNIÈRE AMANDINE

A triple threat for the health conscious, these trout fillets are panfried in butter, drizzled with a browned-butter meunière sauce, and topped with butter-sautéed almonds. It just doesn't get more old New Orleans than that. Always start with room-temperature fish fillets, patted completely dry with paper towels before they are dredged in the flour. That way, the fish will emerge from the pan flaky and crisp at the edges, without sticking or collapsing into a sodden heap. Any mild-flavored, firm-fleshed fillets such as grouper or halibut can be used in this recipe. The dish is also often prepared with soft-shell crabs.

4 trout fillets, about 6 oz (185 g) each

½ cup (2½ oz/75 g) all-purpose (plain) flour

Sea salt and freshly ground pepper

6 tablespoons (3 oz/90 g) unsalted butter

⅓ cup (1½ oz/45 g) sliced flaked almonds

2 tablespoons fresh lemon juice

2 teaspoons Worcestershire sauce

1 lemon, thinly sliced crosswise

1 tablespoon minced fresh flat-leaf (Italian) parsley

Makes 4 servings

1 Remove the trout fillets from the refrigerator about 20 minutes before you begin cooking, to bring them to room temperature. Rinse them well and pat dry gently but thoroughly with paper towels. Spread the flour on a flat plate. Season the fillets on both sides with salt and pepper, then lightly coat with the flour, tapping off the excess.

2 In a large frying pan over medium heat, melt 3 tablespoons of the butter until frothy but not brown. Arrange the fillets in the pan without crowding and cook, turning once, until lightly browned and opaque throughout, 2–3 minutes on each side.

3 Using a wide metal spatula, transfer the fish to a warmed serving platter. Add the remaining 3 tablespoons butter to the pan over medium heat. When it has melted, add the almonds and sauté until lightly browned, about 30 seconds. Immediately add the lemon juice and Worcestershire sauce and stir just until heated through.

4 Remove from the heat. Spoon the almonds and sauce evenly over the fillets. Garnish with lemon slices and sprinkle with the parsley. Serve at once.

Serve with a rich, buttery Chardonnay.

STUFFED CRABS

Here's the traditional destination for leftovers from the Louisiana Seafood Boil (page 115). For the best stuffed crabs, it's necessary to clean them yourself, scraping out all of the tasty yellow fat and orange roe and then using the scrubbed shells for baking the finished dish. Otherwise, you can start with fresh cooked crabmeat—never canned—and mound the stuffing into buttered ramekins. Good Creole cooks also stuff this mixture into halved bell peppers or mirliton squashes (page 186), also known as chayotes, which are first parboiled and then baked until meltingly tender.

1 Preheat the oven to 375°F (190°C). Butter six 1-cup (8–fl oz/250-ml) ramekins. If using boiled crabs, scrub the top shells to hold the stuffing.

2 In a large frying pan over medium heat, warm the ⅓ cup olive oil. Add the yellow onion, celery, bell pepper, garlic, and bay leaves and cook, stirring occasionally, until the onion is tender and golden, 7–8 minutes. Remove the pan from the heat and discard the bay leaves. Stir in the green onions, parsley, thyme, Tabasco, and the 1½ cups bread crumbs. Fold in the crabmeat, being careful not to break up the lumps. Squeeze the lemon juice over the mixture and season well with salt and pepper. Gently stir in the egg.

3 Spoon the mixture into the ramekins or shells, dividing it evenly. Firmly press the remaining ⅓ cup bread crumbs evenly over the tops, then drizzle with the remaining 1 tablespoon olive oil.

4 Arrange the ramekins or shells on a rimmed baking sheet. Bake until puffed and well browned, 30–40 minutes. Serve the stuffed crab warm, straight from the ramekins or shells.

Serve with a dry Riesling or Sauvignon Blanc.

1 lb (500 g) lump crabmeat, picked over to remove any bits of shell or 6 boiled blue crabs cleaned to yield 2 cups (12 oz/375 g) crabmeat

⅓ cup (3 fl oz/80 ml) plus 1 tablespoon olive oil

1 yellow onion, minced

1 celery stalk, minced

½ red bell pepper (capsicum), seeded and minced

2 cloves garlic, minced

2 large bay leaves

¼ cup (¾ oz/20 g) chopped green (spring) onions, including tender green parts

2 tablespoons minced fresh flat-leaf (Italian) parsley

1 teaspoon minced fresh thyme or ¼ teaspoon dried thyme

1 teaspoon Tabasco

1½ cups (3 oz/90 g) plus ⅓ cup (¾ oz/20 g) fresh bread crumbs, preferably from French bread

Juice of ½ lemon

Sea salt and freshly ground pepper

1 large egg, lightly beaten

Makes 6 servings

REDFISH COURTBOUILLON

Because of decades of overfishing during the Cajun blackened fish fad, the lowly redfish has been elevated to stardom and a lofty price. Firm fleshed and meaty, it can easily be substituted, especially in this fragrant stew, by more economical cousins in the drum family, such as black drum or kingfish, or by similarly textured grouper, red snapper, or catfish. Unlike the classic clear broth of France, a courtbouillon in Louisiana or the Caribbean is chunky with tomatoes and tropical seasonings. And in the New Orleans Creole patois, it's pronounced KOO-bee-yon, rather than the French koor-bwee-YON.

2 slices fresh ginger

Zest of ¼ lemon, removed in 2 long strips

2 fresh thyme sprigs

2 large bay leaves

4 tablespoons (4 oz/125 g) unsalted butter

2 yellow onions, halved lengthwise and cut into thin wedges

2 celery stalks, thickly sliced on the diagonal

2 cloves garlic, minced

6 cups (2¼ oz/1.1 kg) peeled and seeded (page 187), then diced ripe tomatoes (5–6 tomatoes)

½ cup (4 fl oz/125 ml) dry white wine

⅛ teaspoon cayenne pepper, or to taste

Sea salt and freshly ground black pepper

4 redfish fillets, 6–8 oz (185–250 g) each

2 tablespoons minced fresh flat-leaf (Italian) parsley

Steamed white rice for serving

Makes 4 servings

1 Crush the ginger slices with the flat side of a knife. Arrange the ginger, lemon zest strips, thyme sprigs, and bay leaves on a small square of cheesecloth (muslin) and secure with kitchen string to make a bouquet garni. Set aside.

2 In a large nonreactive sauté pan with a tight-fitting lid, melt the butter over medium heat. Add the onions and celery and cook, stirring frequently, until the onions are very tender and golden but not browned, 10–12 minutes. Add the garlic and cook, stirring, just until fragrant, about 1 minute.

3 Add the bouquet garni to the pan along with the tomatoes, wine, and cayenne. Raise the heat to medium-high, bring to a boil, and then reduce the heat to low. Cover and simmer gently, stirring occasionally, for 1 hour to blend the flavors. Season well with salt and black pepper. The courtbouillon may be prepared up to this point and refrigerated for up to 2 days. Return it to a simmer before continuing.

4 Season the fish fillets with salt and black pepper. Arrange them on top of the courtbouillon, spooning some of the sauce over the fish. Cover the pan and continue cooking until the fish is translucent and just beginning to flake, 5–10 minutes; the timing will depend on the thickness of the fillets.

5 Discard the bouquet garni. Spoon hot steamed rice into 4 shallow bowls. Using a slotted spoon or spatula, carefully lay the redfish filets over the rice, then ladle plenty of the courtbouillon on top. Sprinkle with the minced parsley and serve.

Serve with a full-bodied amber ale or a dry red Italian wine such as Chianti or Barbera.

GRILLED CHICKEN AND BANANAS WITH WATERMELON RELISH

The long, hot summer is no cause for celebration in Louisiana, but this tropical barbecue cooks so quickly that you can get away from the burning coals and back under the breeze of the ceiling fan in no time. The festive rum-spiked watermelon relish that accompanies it is further cooled by fresh mint. During the nineteenth century, New Orleans was the first United States port of entry for bananas, and the Central and South American imports are still major cargo. Tall, leafy banana trees are a local garden icon and thus, a common sight shading courtyards, porches, and patios.

1 To make the marinade, in a small bowl, whisk together the orange and lemon juices, rum, tamari, peanut oil, brown sugar, and Tabasco until the sugar dissolves. Mix in the ginger and garlic. Place the chicken breasts in a shallow nonreactive dish and pour the marinade evenly over the top, then turn the chicken to coat evenly. Cover and refrigerate for at least 4 hours or up to overnight. Remove from the refrigerator 30 minutes before grilling, to bring to room temperature.

2 About 1 hour before grilling the chicken, make the watermelon relish: In a large bowl, combine the watermelon, onion, mint to taste, chile, rum, and lime juice and toss to combine. Season to taste with salt and pepper. Cover and set aside, stirring occasionally.

3 Prepare a charcoal or gas grill for direct grilling over medium-high heat. Oil the grill rack and place it about 5 inches (13 cm) from the heat source.

4 Remove the chicken from the marinade and discard the marinade. Place the chicken on the grill rack and grill, turning once, until opaque throughout, 4–6 minutes on each side.

5 While the chicken is cooking, remove half of the peel along the length of each banana. Place the bananas, peel side down, on the grill rack and grill until softened, about 5 minutes. Sprinkle the bananas lightly with brown sugar and continue grilling until caramelized, about 5 minutes longer.

6 Transfer the chicken and bananas to individual plates. Place a spoonful of watermelon relish alongside. Pass the remaining relish at the table.

Serve with a big pitcher of lemonade or chilled bottles of pale ale.

FOR THE MARINADE

⅔ cup (5 fl oz/160 ml) fresh orange juice

2 tablespoons *each* fresh lemon juice, dark rum, tamari or soy sauce, and peanut oil

2 tablespoons dark brown sugar, plus more for sprinkling

1 teaspoon Tabasco, or to taste

3 slices fresh ginger, crushed

2 cloves garlic, crushed

4 skinless, boneless chicken breast halves

FOR THE WATERMELON RELISH

3 cups (18 oz/560 g) seeded and finely diced watermelon

2 tablespoons minced sweet onion, such as Vidalia

2–3 tablespoons minced fresh mint, preferably spearmint

1 jalapeño or serrano chile, seeded and minced

2 tablespoons dark rum

1 tablespoon fresh lime juice

Sea salt and freshly ground pepper

4 slightly underripe bananas

Makes 4 servings

CHICKEN CLEMENÇEAU

Imagine a businessman's lunch served at a grand Creole restaurant in the 1940s. It might feature chicken Clemençeau, a rich and meaty dish with a Frenchified flourish of wine and mushrooms that is balanced by a no-nonsense base of home fries and green peas. At once glamorous and homey, the nostalgic sauté is still on the menu at many old-line dining rooms, an enduring favorite that deserves to be revisited. Authenticity requires using a young fowl known as a poussin or a spring chicken, but it is fine to substitute a small fryer, or even skinless, boneless chicken breasts.

1 small young chicken, about
2 lb (1 kg), quartered

Sea salt and freshly ground pepper

3 tablespoons unsalted butter

Canola oil for deep-frying

1 large russet potato, unpeeled,
cut into ½-inch (12-mm) dice

2 cloves garlic, minced

½ lb (250 g) fresh white
mushrooms, wiped clean
and sliced

2 green (spring) onions, including
tender green parts, chopped

⅓ cup (3 fl oz/80 ml) dry
white wine

1½ cups (7½ oz/235 g) small
green peas, fresh or frozen

1 tablespoon minced fresh flat-leaf
(Italian) parsley

Makes 4 servings

1 Preheat the oven to 200°F (95°C). Season the chicken pieces with salt and pepper. In a large, heavy frying pan over medium heat, melt the butter. Working in batches if necessary to avoid crowding, add the chicken, skin side down. Cook until the skin is browned, about 10 minutes. Turn and continue cooking until opaque throughout, about 10 minutes longer. Using tongs, transfer the chicken to a serving platter and keep warm in the oven.

2 While the chicken is cooking, pour oil to a depth of 2 inches (5 cm) into a deep, heavy saucepan or a deep fryer and heat to 350°F (180°C) on a deep-frying thermometer. Add the potato and fry until tender and golden brown, about 10 minutes. Using a slotted spoon, transfer to paper towels to drain.

3 Once the chicken is in the oven, return the frying pan to medium heat, add the garlic, mushrooms, and green onions to the drippings, and sauté until the mushrooms are tender, about 2 minutes. Pour in the wine and deglaze the pan, stirring with a wooden spoon to remove any browned bits from the pan bottom. Add the peas and cook until tender, about 2 minutes. Stir in the fried potatoes and stir and toss just until heated through.

4 Taste and adjust the seasoning. Divide the chicken pieces among warmed plates and spoon the vegetables and sauce over the chicken. Sprinkle with the parsley and serve at once.

Serve with a full-bodied Chardonnay.

BAKED HAM GLAZED WITH CANE SYRUP AND CREOLE MUSTARD

Dorothy Parker once defined eternity as "two people and a ham," but it is possible to speed its departure. After the big Sunday or holiday meal is over and the sandwiches have lost their allure, frugal Louisiana cooks add leftover bits of the meat to gumbos, jambalayas, Cheese Grits Soufflé (page 145), Red Beans and Rice Salad (page 142), or Corn Maque Choux (page 154). And they definitely know how to make good use of the bone, simmering the smoky flavor into a pot of beans or split pea soup for Monday's supper.

1 Preheat the oven to 350°F (180°C). Place the ham, fat side up, on a rack in a roasting pan. Score the top of the ham in a diamond pattern, and stick 1 whole clove into the center of each diamond. If you are using a spiral-sliced ham, use the ground cloves as directed in the next step instead of the whole cloves. Place the ham in the oven and bake for about 15 minutes per pound, or according to the package directions.

2 Meanwhile, in a saucepan over medium heat, combine the cane syrup, brown sugar, mustard, allspice, and the ground cloves, if using. Bring to a boil, stirring to dissolve the sugar, and boil for about 5 minutes, stirring constantly. Generously baste the ham with this glaze every 10 minutes during the final 40 minutes of baking.

3 Remove the ham from the oven and let rest for at least 10 minutes before serving. Slice and serve warm or at room temperature.

Serve with a full-bodied Riesling or Gewürztraminer.

1 precooked boneless ham, 8–10 lb (4–5 kg), rind trimmed away

Whole cloves for inserting, or ¼ teaspoon ground cloves

1 cup (11 oz/345 g) cane syrup or dark molasses

½ cup firmly packed (3½ oz/ 105 g) dark brown sugar

¼ cup (2 oz/60 g) Creole mustard (page 48) or coarse-grain brown mustard

¼ teaspoon ground allspice

Makes 10–12 servings

Raising Cane

Soon after Jesuit missionaries introduced sugarcane to Louisiana in 1751, the banks of the Mississippi were lined with grand manor houses and slave shacks, many of which survive to this day. The plantation system enabled landowners to live like feudal lords, and a popular expression to describe the wealthy was "rich as a sugar planter." For those at the top, it was a sweet life indeed. House parties would last for weeks, the table always set with molasses-glazed hams and other elaborate dishes.

The oldest plantation manor left standing in the Lower Mississippi valley is Destrehan, just west of New Orleans International Airport. The French colonial beauty was built in 1787, and later inhabited by and named for Jean Noel Destrehan, whose brother-in-law Etienne Boré, first mayor of New Orleans, developed the technique for granulating sugar in 1795. Both men were forces in the sugar industry that still thrives in Louisiana, where it contributes some $2 billion annually to the state economy. Real cane syrup is still used here to add a touch of sweetness to everything from baked ham to pecan pie.

DUCK AND ANDOUILLE ÉTOUFFÉE WITH CORN CAKES

Louisiana is nicknamed the Sportsman's Paradise for good reason, and ducks that cross the state along the Great Mississippi Flyway are just asking for trouble. Hunting and fishing have always been serious business, so some of the most flavorful Cajun dishes were created to make the best of wild game. At the Upperline Restaurant in New Orleans, duck is étoufféed (smothered) in a dark and succulent country-style sauce and then served with fluffy corn cakes and sweet-hot pepper jelly. That signature dish was the inspiration for this simpler recipe, which could be served either as a starter or as a main course.

FOR THE ÉTOUFFÉE

Roasted duck and stock (page 100)

½ lb (250 g) andouille sausage

2 *each* yellow onions, celery stalks, and red bell peppers (capsicums)

½ cup (4 fl oz/125 ml) corn oil

½ cup (2½ oz/75 g) all-purpose (plain) flour

2 cloves garlic, minced

2 tablespoons tomato paste

¼ teaspoon cayenne pepper

2 teaspoons *each* chopped fresh thyme and oregano

2 bay leaves

FOR THE CORN CAKES

5–6 green (spring) onions

1¼ cups (6½ oz/200 g) cornmeal

⅓ cup (2 oz/60 g) all-purpose (plain) flour

1¼ teaspoons sea salt

½ teaspoon baking soda (bicarbonate of soda)

1 large egg, at room temperature

2 cups (16 fl oz/500 ml) buttermilk

3 tablespoons butter, melted

Hot-Pepper Jelly (page 158)

Makes 6 servings

1 To make the étouffée, roast the duck and make the duck stock as directed in Duck and Wild Mushroom Gumbo. Coarsely shred the duck meat and set aside. Discard the skin. Pour the strained duck stock into a saucepan, bring to a boil over high heat, and boil until reduced to 4 cups (32 fl oz/1 l), 10 minutes. Set aside.

2 Finely chop the andouille and set aside. Finely chop the onions, celery, and bell peppers and set aside. Heat a large, heavy frying pan, preferably cast iron, over medium-high heat just until it begins to smoke. Add the oil and then whisk in the flour and continue whisking constantly until you have a dark brown roux, 3–5 minutes. Add the onions, celery, bell peppers, and andouille and cook, stirring constantly, until very tender and browned, 5–7 minutes. Add the garlic and cook, stirring, for 2 minutes longer. Add the warm duck stock and the tomato paste and stir until incorporated. Add the cayenne, thyme, oregano, and bay leaves, bring to a boil, and boil for 10 minutes. Reduce the heat to maintain a lively simmer, cover, and cook, stirring occasionally, for 1 hour. Using a large spoon, skim off any excess oil from the surface.

3 Add the shredded duck meat to the sauce. Season to taste with salt and pepper. Raise the heat to medium-high, bring the mixture to a boil, and then reduce the heat to medium-low and simmer, uncovered, for 15 minutes to heat the duck meat and again blend the flavors. Taste and adjust the seasoning and discard the bay leaves. Remove from the heat, cover, and keep warm.

4 To make the corn cakes, finely chop the green onions, including the tender green parts, and set aside. Preheat a large cast-iron frying pan over medium-high heat or preheat an electric griddle to 375°F (190°C). When the surface is hot, grease generously with butter or canola oil.

5 While the pan is heating, in a large bowl, whisk together the cornmeal, flour, salt, and baking soda until blended. Make a well in the center. In a separate bowl, beat the egg. Beat in the buttermilk and melted butter. Add to the dry ingredients and stir gently just until incorporated. Add the green onions and stir again.

6 When the pan is hot, for each corn cake, scoop up a scant ¼ cup (2 fl oz/60 ml) of the batter and pour onto the hot surface. The batter will spread slightly, so keep the cakes well spaced. Fry until the edges appear dry and lightly browned, 1–2 minutes. Turn the cakes over and again fry until the edges appear lightly browned, 1–2 minutes longer. Transfer to a warmed platter to keep warm. Repeat with the remaining batter. You should have 18 corn cakes.

7 To serve, reheat the étouffée if necessary. Fan 3 corn cakes on each warmed individual plate and ladle the hot étouffée alongside and over the cakes. Serve at once. Pass the hot-pepper jelly at the table.

Serve with a peppery red wine such as Zinfandel.

GARLIC PORK ROAST

Pork is a mainstay in Louisiana cooking, from the andouille sausage in gumbo to the chopped ham that seasons old-fashioned smothered garden vegetables. Greens are cooked in bacon fat, and crisp fried cracklins are crumbled into corn bread. However, the lean center-cut loin is reserved for special occasions. It is usually stuffed with garlic, which can taste unpleasantly sharp, especially when the meat is slowly cooked at a low temperature, as it is here, to keep it tender and moist. A "wet rub" of roasted garlic and fresh herbs solves that problem, and it adds even more flavor as the roast marinates overnight.

1 Preheat the oven or toaster oven to 350°F (180°C). Peel away as much of the thin, papery skin covering the garlic head as possible while leaving it intact. Using a sharp knife, cut about ½ inch (12 mm) from the top of the head, exposing the cloves. Place the garlic, cut side up, in a small baking dish. Sprinkle the cut surface with the cayenne and then drizzle with 1 tablespoon of the olive oil. Bake the garlic until it is soft when pierced with the tip of a knife and browned, about 30 minutes. Remove from the oven and let cool to room temperature.

2 Meanwhile, in a frying pan over medium heat, warm the remaining 2 tablespoons olive oil. Add the yellow onion and sauté until tender and golden, about 10 minutes. Stir in the sage and thyme. Remove from the heat.

3 Separate the cloves from the garlic head and squeeze the pulp into the oil remaining in the baking dish. Using a fork, mash the pulp and oil together to make a paste. You should have about 1 heaping tablespoon. Add the paste to the onion mixture in the frying pan and stir to blend. Season to taste with salt and black pepper.

4 Trim the pork loin so that only about ¼ inch (6 mm) of fat remains. Season it well with black pepper. With the fat side up, use a chef's knife to make about 15 slits in the surface of the meat, making them about 1 inch (2.5 cm) deep and 1 inch long and spacing them evenly. Stuff most of the garlic mixture into the slits and rub the remainder on the surface of the roast. Place the pork loin in a dish, cover tightly, and refrigerate for at least 8 hours or up to 24 hours.

5 Preheat the oven to 300°F (150°C). Remove the pork loin from the refrigerator and place, fat side up, in a roasting pan. Season with salt and black pepper and set aside for 30 minutes, to bring to room temperature.

6 Roast the pork loin, uncovered, until an instant-read thermometer inserted into the thickest part of the roast away from the bone registers 160°–165°F (71°–74°C). Remove from the oven, transfer to a platter away from any drafts, and let rest for about 5 minutes before carving.

Serve with a fruity Pinot Noir or a medium-bodied Bordeaux.

1 head garlic

⅛ teaspoon cayenne pepper

3 tablespoons olive oil

1 yellow onion, finely chopped

1 tablespoon finely chopped fresh sage

1 tablespoon coarsely chopped fresh thyme

Sea salt and freshly ground black pepper

1 boneless center-cut pork loin, 4 lb (2 kg)

Makes 8–10 servings

VEAL GRILLADES WITH GRITS

In Cajun country, grillades (pronounced GREE-yods) are typically thin scallops of pork or beef round steak, simmered in a rich brown gravy and served for breakfast or lunch. In New Orleans, they are bathed in a spicier Creole sauce colored by tomatoes, and the meat is more likely to be veal, especially in fine restaurants, where they are a classic weekend brunch dish served with creamy hominy grits. This version comes from one of the city's top young chefs, Richard Benz, who, with his wife, owns and operates Dick and Jenny's in a lively Uptown cottage on Tchoupitoulas Street.

4 cups (32 fl oz/1 l) chicken stock

1 cup (6 oz/185 g) old-fashioned
or quick grits

6 tablespoons (2 oz/60 g)
all-purpose (plain) flour

Sea salt and freshly ground pepper

12 veal cutlets, about
5 oz (155 g) each

¼ cup (2 fl oz/60 ml) corn oil

1 yellow onion, thinly sliced

1 celery stalk, finely chopped

1 red or green bell pepper
(capsicum), seeded and chopped

1 large tomato, peeled and seeded
(page 187), then chopped

1 small clove garlic, minced

1 tablespoon tomato paste

1½ cups (12 fl oz/375 ml)
beef stock

1 tablespoon fresh thyme

Makes 6 servings

1 In a saucepan over high heat, bring the chicken stock to a boil. Stir in the grits, reduce the heat to low, cover, and cook, stirring occasionally, until thick and creamy, 15–20 minutes for old-fashioned grits or 5–6 minutes for quick grits.

2 Meanwhile, preheat the oven to 250°F (120°C) and place an ovenproof platter in it. On a plate, stir together 4 tablespoons (1½ oz/45 g) of the flour, ½ teaspoon salt, and ¼ teaspoon pepper. Lightly coat the veal cutlets on both sides with the seasoned flour, tapping off the excess.

3 In a large frying pan over medium heat, warm the oil. Working in batches, add the cutlets and brown on both sides, about 2 minutes on each side. Transfer the cutlets to the platter in the oven to keep warm.

4 When all the cutlets are browned, return the pan to medium heat and add the onion, celery, bell pepper, tomato, and garlic to the drippings. Cook, stirring, until tender, about 5 minutes. Add the tomato paste and mix well. Stir in the remaining 2 tablespoons

flour, mixing well. Add the beef stock and thyme and whisk to blend. Raise the heat to high, bring to a boil, and then reduce the heat to medium-low. Simmer, stirring frequently, for 5 minutes to blend the flavors. Season to taste with salt and pepper.

5 Add the browned cutlets to the pan and spoon the sauce over them. Simmer for 5 minutes longer to heat through.

6 Taste and adjust the seasoning. Spoon the hot grits onto warmed individual plates and spoon the grillades and sauce over the top. Serve at once.

Serve with a Pouilly-Fuissé or other crisp white wine.

MUFFULETTA

Named for the bread introduced to America by Sicilian immigrants in the early 1900s, this hubcap-sized sandwich is a New Orleans icon, a four-fisted feast for two. Variations on the muffuletta, sold for generations at Central and Progress groceries (two neighboring delis in the French Quarter), now appear on menus throughout the region. To heat or not to heat, that is the controversy. This is a broiled version. For an authentic muffuletta, do not toast the bread, and place the olive salad on top of the other ingredients, above the cheese.

1 To make the olive salad, in a bowl, toss together the olives, *giardiniera,* celery, garlic, and oregano to combine. Add the olive oil and toss again. Set aside at room temperature for at least 30 minutes or up to 2 days to allow the flavors to blend.

2 Preheat the broiler (grill). Split the bread in half horizontally. Generously brush the cut sides with oil from the olive salad. On the bottom half of the bread stack the ham, salami, and mortadella (if using). Top with the chopped olive salad and then the cheese. Place on a rimmed baking sheet. Place the top half of the loaf, cut side up, next to the filled bottom half.

3 Slip the baking sheet under the broiler about 5 inches (13 cm) from the heat source and broil (grill) until the meats are warmed, the cheese is melted, and the bread is lightly toasted, 3–5 minutes.

4 Remove from the broiler and carefully transfer the bottom half to a cutting board. Replace the top half of the bread and cut the sandwich into 4 wedges. Serve at once.

Serve with Barq's Root Beer, the traditional accompaniment, or a rustic Italian table wine such as Lambrusco.

FOR THE CHOPPED OLIVE SALAD

¾ cup (5 oz/155 g) drained and coarsely chopped pimiento-stuffed green olives

⅓ cup (2 oz/60 g) drained and finely chopped mild pickled *giardiniera* of cauliflower, carrots, and cocktail onions

1 small celery stalk, preferably from the heart, finely chopped

1 clove garlic, minced

1 teaspoon minced fresh oregano or ¼ teaspoon dried oregano

3 tablespoons extra-virgin olive oil

8-inch (20-cm) muffuletta loaf or other round, crusty, seeded Italian loaf

4–6 oz (125–185 g) thinly sliced ham

2–3 oz (60–90 g) thinly sliced Genoa salami

¼ lb (125 g) sliced mortadella sausage or other Italian cold cuts (optional)

¼ lb (125 g) sliced Provolone cheese

Makes 4 servings

Mood Music

To taste the Sicilian roots of brassy Bourbon Street jazz, serve your muffuletta to music by Italian American swingers Al Belletto, Sam Butera, Sharky Bonano, or the raspy "Just a Gigolo" voice of favorite son Louis Prima.

Long after Louis Armstrong blew his horn on "Struttin' with Some Barbecue," the tune was taken up by a new generation of musicians, including trumpeter Kermit Ruffins, who has been known to fire up his grill outside clubs to cook for fans before a show. R&B diva Irma Thomas sometimes gets behind the stove at her lounge, The Lion's Den, fortifying patrons with red beans and rice.

Elvis croons an ode to crawfish in the film *King Creole,* while Dr. John works his weird magic on songs like "Croaker Courtbouillon." Out in Cajun country, accordionist Terrance Simien wails, *"Zydeco son pas salé. Moi su pas tracasser"* (The snap beans are not salty. I am not worried). And every chank-a-chank band in every roadhouse knows "Jambalaya, crawfish pie, et filé gumbo, 'cause tonight I'm going to see my chère amie–oh."

VEGETABLES AND SIDES

Kitchen tables in Louisiana get plenty of color from sweet potatoes, eggplant,

juicy Creole tomatoes, sweet summer corn, green beans, and spicy jambalaya.

Many side dishes are substantial enough to serve as main courses in Louisiana, which supplies much of the nation's rice and sweet potatoes, two essential staples of New Orleans kitchens. Natives also love those Old South oddities: grits and okra. Home gardeners are most likely to grow bell peppers (capsicums), eggplants (aubergines), tomatoes, and mirlitons. Vegetarians will be dismayed to find sausage or ham seasoning everything from green beans to smothered cabbage, but even those standards are changing, as modern cooks have come to appreciate fresh, crisp vegetables on their own.

ZYDECO BEANS WITH BRABANT POTATOES

Oddly enough, the raucous African-Cajun sound called zydeco, born in Louisiana and heard around the world, got its name from plain old green beans. According to musician Clifton Chenier, family and friends would gather on the front porch each Sunday, where some syncopated on squeeze boxes and washboards while others snapped beans for dinner. They called it les haricots (bean) music, pronounced in the regional dialect as zydeco. Here, the beans are flavored with ginger and garlic and paired with butter-crisped brabant-style potatoes, which can also be served on their own with grilled meats.

1 In a large frying pan with a tight-fitting lid, combine the potatoes, ginger, bay leaf, and stock over high heat. Bring to a boil, reduce the heat to medium-low, cover, and simmer until the potatoes are tender but still firm when pierced with the tip of a knife, about 10 minutes. Using a slotted spoon, transfer the potatoes to a colander to drain. Pat the potatoes dry with paper towels and set aside.

2 Add the green beans to the liquid remaining in the frying pan over medium-high heat. Bring to a boil, reduce the heat to low, cover, and simmer until the green beans are tender-crisp, 6–7 minutes. Drain in a colander and discard the stock, ginger, and bay leaf. Set the green beans aside.

3 Preheat the oven to 200°F (95°C). Wipe the frying pan dry, return it to medium-high heat, and add 2 tablespoons of the butter. When the butter melts, add the potatoes, season to taste with salt and pepper, and toss until browned and crisp on all sides, about 5 minutes. Transfer the potatoes to an ovenproof bowl and keep warm in the oven.

4 Return the frying pan to medium-high heat and melt the remaining 1 tablespoon butter. Add the onion and garlic and sauté until tender but not browned, about 2 minutes. Add the green beans, season to taste with salt and pepper, and toss until heated through, 1–2 minutes.

5 Add the warm potatoes, then taste and adjust the seasoning. Transfer to a warmed serving dish and serve at once.

8 small red or white new potatoes, unpeeled, halved

2 large slices fresh ginger

1 bay leaf

3 cups (24 fl oz/750 ml) chicken stock

½ lb (250 g) young, tender green beans

3 tablespoons unsalted butter

Sea salt and freshly ground pepper

1 small red onion, halved lengthwise and very thinly sliced

1 clove garlic, minced

Makes 4–6 servings

RED BEANS AND RICE SALAD

The tradition of eating red beans and rice for Monday night supper in New Orleans is so ingrained in the collective food consciousness that this dish has become the emblem of Crescent City cooking, even inspiring native son Louis Armstrong to sign his correspondence "Red beans and ricely yours." Transformed into a cool and portable salad, it is just right for tailgate parties, Mardi Gras parades, or picnics. Although you could substitute about 3 cups (21 oz/655 g) canned beans that have been drained and rinsed, the resulting flavor and texture is much better if you cook them from scratch.

1 cup (7 oz/220 g) dried red kidney beans

2 whole cloves

1 yellow onion

4 cloves garlic, unpeeled

2 bay leaves

3 cups (24 fl oz/750 ml) chicken stock or water

½ teaspoon *each* sea salt and sugar

2 tablespoons cider vinegar

1 teaspoon *each* Creole mustard or coarse-grain brown mustard and Tabasco, plus more for serving

1 teaspoon minced fresh thyme, plus sprigs for garnish

⅓ cup (3 fl oz/80 ml) olive oil

Freshly ground pepper

2 large ripe tomatoes

1 *each* celery stalk, green bell pepper (capsicum), and small red onion

¼ lb (125 g) cooked ham (optional)

¼ cup (⅓ oz/10 g) minced fresh flat-leaf (Italian) parsley leaves

3 cups (15 oz/470 g) steamed long-grain white rice

Makes 8–10 servings

1 Pick over the beans and discard any misshapen beans or stones. Rinse the beans and drain. Place in a bowl, add plenty of cold water to cover, and let soak for several hours or overnight.

2 Drain the beans and place them in a saucepan. Stick the cloves into the yellow onion and add it to the saucepan along with the garlic, bay leaves, and stock. Place over high heat, bring to a boil, reduce the heat to maintain a lively simmer, cover, and cook until the beans are just tender but not mushy, about 1 hour. Drain and reserve the beans and garlic cloves separately; discard the onion and bay leaves. (The beans may be cooked and stored, tightly covered, in the refrigerator for up to 2 days in advance.)

3 Squeeze the cooked garlic cloves out of the skins, releasing the pulp into a large serving bowl and discarding the skins. Mash the garlic with the salt and sugar and then whisk in the vinegar until the salt and sugar have dissolved. Whisk in the mustard, Tabasco, minced thyme, and olive oil until blended. Add several grinds of pepper. Set aside for at least 30 minutes to allow the flavors to blend. Taste and adjust the seasoning. Whisk again before continuing.

4 Cut the tomatoes in half crosswise. Holding each half cut side down over the sink, squeeze gently to force out the seeds. Use a fingertip, if necessary, to dislodge them. Finely chop the tomatoes. Thinly slice the celery stalk. Halve the bell pepper, remove the stem, seeds, and ribs, and chop finely. Finely chop the red onion. Finely dice the ham, if using.

5 Add the tomatoes, celery, bell pepper, red onion, parsley, ham (if using), drained beans, and rice to the serving bowl. Toss gently to combine. Set aside at room temperature for at least 30 minutes or up to 2 hours.

6 Before serving, taste and adjust the seasoning. Garnish with thyme sprigs and serve at room temperature. Pass a bottle of Tabasco at the table.

CHEESE GRITS SOUFFLÉ

Despite what you may have read in community cookbooks, this Southern classic doesn't have to be made with a block of Velveeta or a roll of processed garlic cheese (although either would be authentic). You might also try Gruyère, mild Colby, or pepper Jack. It is the quintessential brunch dish, often enriched by crumbled crisp bacon or bits of browned sausage. It is also a fine accompaniment for the Baked Ham Glazed with Cane Syrup and Creole Mustard (page 127) or Garlic Pork Roast (page 131).

1 In a saucepan over high heat, bring 4 cups (32 fl oz/1 l) water and ½ teaspoon salt to a boil. Stir in the grits and return to a boil. Reduce the heat to very low and simmer, stirring frequently, until thick and creamy, 15–20 minutes for old-fashioned grits or 5–6 minutes for quick grits. Remove the pan from the heat. Add the butter, cayenne, and cheese and stir until the cheese is melted and smooth. Stir in the green onions and let cool until lukewarm. Add the egg yolks and stir until blended.

2 While the grits are cooking, preheat the oven to 350°F (180°C). Generously butter a 9-by-13-inch (23-by-33-cm) baking dish.

3 In a large bowl, using an electric mixer on high speed, beat the egg whites until they form glossy peaks. Fold about one-fourth of the beaten egg whites into the grits to lighten the mixture, then gently fold in the remaining whites. Pour the mixture into the prepared baking dish.

4 Bake until puffed and golden brown, about 45 minutes. Serve at once, directly from the dish.

Sea salt

1 cup (6 oz/185 g) old-fashioned or quick grits

4 tablespoons (2 oz/60 g) unsalted butter

¼ teaspoon cayenne pepper

1 cup (4 oz/125 g) finely shredded sharp Cheddar cheese

½ cup (1½ oz/45 g) chopped green (spring) onions, including tender green parts

4 large eggs, separated

Makes 4–6 servings

Creole Brunch

Long before the idea was taken up by the rest of the country as a social event for late sleepers, Sunday brunch was firmly established in New Orleans. In this traditionally Catholic city, the faithful were required to fast before receiving Holy Communion, so when hungry parishioners were released around noon after Sunday Mass, the streets would be filled with vendors peddling hot calas (page 174), beignets (page 181), and other temptations to fuel the walk home, where a larger meal awaited.

The custom wasn't limited to weekends. In the 1850s, Marie Abadie Tujague opened the still-popular Tujague's and soon earned a national reputation with the elaborate late-morning breakfasts she served to French Market workers.

By the 1950s, the famous Breakfast at Brennan's had put another local restaurant on the culinary map. And later, Dick Brennan originated the much-imitated jazz brunch at Commander's Palace in 1975. This recent tradition has also inspired gospel brunches, blues brunches, Broadway brunches, and other extravaganzas across the country.

STUFFED ARTICHOKES

In the eighteenth century, the downtown Warehouse-Arts District of New Orleans was planted with fields of artichokes. This tasty preparation arrived later, around the late nineteenth century, with the Sicilian immigrants who have influenced local cooking and culture ever since. Lemony steamed artichokes, interleaved with seasoned bread crumbs and olive oil, are standard fare at casual neighborhood restaurants, where it's customary for two diners to order one to share. Just pluck out a leaf and use your teeth to scrape off the tangy pulp and moist stuffing.

2 cups (4 oz/125 g) fresh bread crumbs, preferably from French bread (page 185)

½ cup (2 oz/60 g) grated Parmesan cheese

2 tablespoons minced fresh flat-leaf (Italian) parsley leaves

1 teaspoon minced fresh thyme

1 teaspoon minced fresh oregano

⅓ cup (3 fl oz/80 ml) olive oil

3 cloves garlic, minced

Sea salt and freshly ground pepper

2 large artichokes, about ½ lb (250 g) each

1 lemon wedge plus 2 thin lemon slices

Juice of 1 lemon

Makes 4 servings

1 In a bowl, stir together the bread crumbs, Parmesan, parsley, thyme, and oregano. In a small frying pan over medium-low heat, warm the olive oil. Add the garlic and sauté until tender and fragrant but not at all browned, 2–3 minutes. Add to the bread crumb mixture, tossing to blend well. Season generously with salt and pepper. Set aside.

2 Using a stainless-steel knife, cut off the top 2 inches (5 cm) from 1 artichoke. Immediately rub the cut edges with the lemon wedge to prevent discoloration. Trim off the stem, flush with the bottom, so that the artichoke will stand upright on a plate. Pull off the small dark leaves around the base, and then use kitchen shears to clip the thorny points from all the other leaves. Rub the cut edges with the lemon wedge. Using a spoon, scoop out the feathery "choke" at the center of the artichoke. Repeat with the remaining artichoke.

3 Starting at the center, pack half of the bread crumb mixture into the scooped out center and between the rows of leaves of one artichoke. (It helps to have one person to spread the leaves while another spoons in the bread crumbs.) Repeat with the second artichoke, then top each with a lemon slice.

4 Stand the stuffed artichokes in a nonreactive pot. Add water to a depth of 1 inch (2.5 cm) and the juice of 1 lemon. Cover the pot, place over high heat, bring to a boil, and then reduce the heat to low. Begin checking for doneness after 30 minutes. The artichokes are done when you can easily pull out a leaf and the bottoms are easily pierced with the tip of a knife.

5 Remove the artichokes from the pot and let stand for at least 10 minutes before serving warm or at room temperature. Each artichoke serves two.

DIRTY RICE

Beyond the state line, this dish is better known by inoffensive names like "Cajun rice" or "rice dressing." But the Big Easy is not for those who are easily offended, and neither is this recipe, which is made with ground chicken gizzards and livers and plenty of onions and garlic. It is fine to substitute an equal amount of beef chuck or pork shoulder meat for the organ meats, but the grinding is essential to distribute the flavors evenly and give the dish its characteristic "dirty" appearance. A fixture at family reunions and church suppers, it tastes much better than it sounds.

1 Using a meat grinder, grind the gizzards and livers. Alternatively, place the gizzards and livers in a food processor and pulse briefly until the mixture is chopped but not puréed, about 5 seconds.

2 In a large, heavy frying pan, preferably cast iron, melt the butter over medium heat. Add the ground gizzards and livers, yellow onions, celery, bell pepper, garlic, and cayenne. Season with salt and black pepper. Sauté, stirring, for 1–2 minutes. Reduce the heat to medium-low and continue cooking, stirring frequently, until the vegetables are browned and very tender, the whole mixture is cooked through, and the flavors have melded, about 45 minutes.

3 Meanwhile, in a 1½-qt (1.5-l) saucepan over high heat, bring the stock to a boil. Stir in the rice and return to a boil. Reduce the heat to low, cover, and cook for 20 minutes. After 20 minutes, uncover and check to see if the liquid is absorbed and the rice is tender. If not, re-cover and cook for a few minutes longer. Remove from the heat and set aside to rest, still covered, for about 10 minutes.

4 Add the green onions and parsley to the meat mixture and cook, stirring frequently until the green onions are softened, about 5 minutes. Add the rice and cook, stirring frequently, until heated through and well blended, 3–5 minutes.

5 Taste and adjust the seasoning. Transfer to a warmed serving bowl and serve at once.

½ lb (250 g) chicken gizzards

½ lb (250 g) chicken livers

4 tablespoons (2 oz/60 g) unsalted butter

2 large yellow onions, finely chopped

2 celery stalks, finely chopped

1 red bell pepper (capsicum), seeded and finely chopped

4 cloves garlic, minced

⅛ teaspoon cayenne pepper, or more to taste

Sea salt and freshly ground black pepper

2 cups (16 fl oz/500 ml) chicken stock

1 cup (5 oz/155 g) long-grain white rice

6 green (spring) onions, including tender green parts, thinly sliced

⅓ cup (⅓ oz/10 g) minced fresh flat-leaf (Italian) parsley leaves

Makes 10–12 servings

CREOLE TOMATO GRATIN

Buttered bread crumbs crisp into a simple, wonderful crust on this old-fashioned gratin of herb-spiked tomatoes. Worth heating the oven on a summer day, it's a fine centerpiece for a meatless meal from the garden or farmers' market, accompanied by Corn Maque Choux (page 154), Zydeco Beans with Brabant Potatoes (page 141), and French-Fried Eggplant (page 70). To peel fresh tomatoes, using a sharp knife, just make an X on the bottom of the tomato and then blanch them in boiling water for 30 seconds. You'll be able to slip the skins right off with your fingers.

5 tablespoons (2½ oz/75 g) unsalted butter

2 cloves garlic, minced

2 cups (4 oz/125 g) fresh bread crumbs, preferably from French bread (page 185)

4 ripe Creole or beefsteak tomatoes, peeled and cut into slices ½ inch (12 mm) thick

Sea salt and freshly ground pepper

2 tablespoons minced fresh basil

2 tablespoons minced fresh flat-leaf (Italian) parsley leaves

2 tablespoons grated Parmesan cheese

Makes 4 servings

1 Preheat the oven to 350°F (180°C). Butter a gratin dish or other shallow dish about 11 inches (28 cm) long and 9 inches (23 cm) wide.

2 In a frying pan over medium-low heat, melt the butter. Add the garlic and sauté until tender and fragrant but not at all browned, 2–3 minutes. Remove from the heat and stir in the bread crumbs until evenly coated with the butter mixture.

3 Spread about one-fourth of the bread crumb mixture evenly in the bottom of the prepared gratin dish. Top with half of the tomatoes, arranging them in a single layer with the slices overlapping.

Sprinkle with salt, pepper, and 1 tablespoon each of the basil and parsley. Top with one-third of the remaining bread crumb mixture, and then the remaining tomatoes. Sprinkle with salt and pepper, and the remaining basil and parsley. Top with the remaining bread crumb mixture, and sprinkle the Parmesan evenly on the top.

4 Bake, uncovered, until browned and bubbly, about 1 hour. Serve hot, directly from the dish.

EGGPLANT JAMBALAYA

Another signature dish of Louisiana, jambalaya is usually rich and meaty. In New Orleans and along the coastal bayous, the seasoned rice might contain shrimp and tomatoes. On the prairies of Cajun country, it's more likely to contain chicken and sausage. This nontraditional recipe features eggplant instead and could easily be made vegetarian if you leave out the ham. Similar to paella, jambalaya exhibits a Spanish influence, but it also has strong roots in Africa, where a spicy meat and vegetable sauté is known as a jambé, and ya means rice.

1 In a deep nonreactive sauté pan with a tight-fitting lid, warm the oil over medium heat. Add the yellow onion, bell pepper, celery, and the ham, if using, and sauté, stirring frequently, until the vegetables are very tender and lightly browned, 10–15 minutes.

2 Add the garlic, bay leaves, oregano, thyme, and cayenne and cook, stirring, just until the garlic releases its fragrance, about 2 minutes. Add ½ cup (1½ oz/45 g) of the green onions, the eggplant, tomatoes, stock, and rice. Stir well and season with salt and black pepper. Raise the heat to medium-high, bring to a boil, and then immediately reduce the heat to low. Stir well, scraping the pan bottom to be sure nothing sticks. Cover tightly and cook, without stirring, for 20 minutes. Uncover and check to see if the liquid is absorbed and the rice is tender. If not, re-cover and cook for a few minutes longer.

3 Remove the pan from the heat and set aside to let stand, still covered, for 5 minutes. Discard the bay leaves and stir lightly with a fork to fluff before serving. Garnish with the remaining green onions.

¼ cup (2 fl oz/60 ml) olive oil

1 yellow onion, finely chopped

1 red or yellow bell pepper (capsicum), seeded and finely chopped

2 celery stalks, finely chopped

½ lb (250 g) smoked ham, cut into ½-inch (12-mm) dice (optional)

3 cloves garlic, minced

2 large bay leaves

1½ teaspoons minced fresh oregano

1 teaspoon minced fresh thyme

¼ teaspoon cayenne pepper

¾ cup (2 oz/60 g) chopped green (spring) onions, including tender green parts

1 small eggplant (aubergine), about ½ lb (250 g), peeled and cut into ½-inch (12-mm) dice

1 can (14 oz/440 g) diced tomatoes, with juice

1½ cups (12 fl oz/375 ml) chicken or vegetable stock

1 cup (7 oz/220 g) uncooked long-grain white rice

Sea salt and ground black pepper

Makes 6 servings

Cooking with Cast Iron

Trendy gadgets may come and go, but one item has always been essential in Louisiana kitchens: a big cast-iron frying pan that sizzles eggs and andouille for breakfast and fried chicken for dinner. In addition, many cooks depend on a smaller frying pan for crisp-edged corn bread and a deeper Dutch oven for stews, gumbos, and jambalayas. Cast-iron corn-stick pans and muffin pans are also common. All are great at conducting and maintaining even heat. The dark surface is perfect for searing or deep-frying, although unsuitable for cooking acidic tomato or wine sauces.

These workhorses can be passed down for generations, burnished to a black sheen that comes only with years of use. Those who have not inherited a pan can purchase preseasoned cast-iron cookware. Or, you can "season" it yourself by coating the interior with solid vegetable shortening and putting it in a 350°F (180°C) oven for 1 hour. This simple process allows the iron to absorb the oil, creating a natural nonstick finish. The gray pan will first darken to a streaky caramel, then blacken over time.

CORN MAQUE CHOUX

The influence of the Choctaws, native to the area around New Orleans, is evident in this traditional Cajun stir-fry, a casual farmhouse jumble that is so much more than the sum of its parts. Also known as maquechoux, it is a specialty throughout southeast Louisiana, where every cook has a favorite version. Some include cream, crisp bacon, ham, or shellfish. Fresh sweet corn, however, is essential, and simplicity is always best when summer gardens are at their peak. Many older recipes produce a long-simmering and rather sludgy stew, but here the fresh flavors and bright colors are free to shine.

6 ears corn, husked

3 tablespoons unsalted butter

1 yellow onion, chopped

1 green bell pepper (capsicum), seeded and chopped

2 ripe tomatoes, peeled and seeded (page 187), then chopped

Sea salt and freshly ground black pepper

Cayenne pepper

Makes 4–6 servings

1 In a large, shallow bowl, stand 1 ear of corn upright, stem end down. Using a large, sharp knife, slice downward to remove all the kernels, giving the ear a quarter turn after each cut. Then, using the back of the knife, scrape the cob downward in the same fashion, releasing the creamy "milk." Repeat with the remaining ears. Discard the cobs and set the corn kernels and their milk aside.

2 In a large frying pan over medium heat, melt the butter. Add the onion and bell pepper and sauté, stirring frequently, until very tender and lightly browned, 10–15 minutes. Add the tomatoes and the corn kernels and their milk and stir just until the kernels are tender-crisp, 2–3 minutes. Season well with salt, black pepper, and cayenne. Spoon into a warmed serving bowl and serve at once.

SUGARCANE RUM–GLAZED SWEET POTATOES

Following the Old South dictum that food can never be too rich or too sweet, canned-yam dishes are commonly smothered in sugar, margarine, and tiny marshmallows. Here, just enough butter and cane syrup are used to add a festive gloss while the flavor of the freshly baked sweet potatoes shines through, helped along with a couple shots of pure sugarcane rum. Many cooks elsewhere boil the sweet potatoes, but it's best to bake them in the oven, which enhances their natural sugars and increases their syrupy juices. Never wrap them in aluminum foil or they'll emerge with mushy flesh and limp skins.

1 Preheat the oven to 400°F (200°C). Scrub the potatoes, then dry well. Place on a rimmed baking sheet or directly on the oven rack and bake for 15 minutes. Reduce the oven temperature to 375°F (190°C) and continue to bake until tender when pierced with a fork but not mushy, 35–40 minutes. Remove from the oven, let cool for 5–10 minutes, then peel the potatoes. (You can make the recipe up to this point and cover and refrigerate the peeled potatoes for up to 2 days before continuing.) Reduce the oven temperature to 350°F (180°C).

2 Generously butter a 9-by-13-inch (23-by-33-cm) gratin dish or rectangular baking dish. Cut the cooled potatoes into slices ½ inch (12 mm) thick. Arrange the slices in 2 layers in the prepared dish.

3 In a small saucepan over medium heat, melt the butter with the cane syrup, lemon zest and juice, ginger, and nutmeg. Remove the pan from the heat, add the rum, and stir until smooth. Pour over the layered potatoes.

4 Bake, uncovered, until the potatoes are lightly browned around the edges and the sauce is hot and bubbly, 30–40 minutes. Serve at once, directly from the dish.

6 sweet potatoes, about 4 lb (2 kg) total weight, unpeeled

4 tablespoons (2 oz/60 g) unsalted butter

¼ cup (2 fl oz/60 ml) cane syrup

1 teaspoon grated lemon zest

2 teaspoons fresh lemon juice

½ teaspoon ground ginger

¼ teaspoon freshly grated nutmeg

¼ cup (2 fl oz/60 ml) sugarcane rum such as New Orleans or Mount Gay

Makes 8–10 servings

IRON-SKILLET CORN BREAD WITH HOT-PEPPER JELLY

This is old-fashioned Louisiana corn bread, dense and grainy, with no sugar and a slight tang from the buttermilk. An iron skillet or frying pan is not essential (any ovenproof pan will work), although it is traditional in the South for this dish. Many cooks still use rendered bacon fat in place of the oil, crumbling the crisp bacon into the batter. The pepper jelly is another regional specialty that is also wonderful on biscuits or peanut butter sandwiches; drizzled over cream cheese; or as a glaze for ham, pork roast, or grilled chicken. Use jalapeños for a milder jelly, serranos if you prefer it hotter.

FOR THE HOT-PEPPER JELLY

1 red, 1 green, and 1 yellow bell pepper (capsicum), seeded and coarsely chopped

4–6 jalapeño or serrano chiles, seeded and coarsely chopped

6½ cups (3¼ lb/1.6 kg) sugar

1½ cups (12 fl oz/375 ml) cane vinegar or cider vinegar

1 bottle (6–7 fl oz/180–220 ml) liquid pectin

FOR THE CORN BREAD

⅓ cup (3 fl oz/80 ml) corn oil

1⅔ cups (8½ oz/265 g) yellow cornmeal

⅓ cup (2 oz/60 g) all-purpose (plain) flour

1 teaspoon sea salt

1 teaspoon baking powder

½ teaspoon baking soda (bicarbonate of soda)

3 large eggs

2 cups (16 fl oz/500 ml) buttermilk

Makes 8–12 servings

1 To make the hot-pepper jelly, place 6 half-pint (8–fl oz/250-ml) jars in a large kettle, cover with water, bring to a boil, and boil for 10 minutes. Remove from the heat and let the jars stand in the water until ready to fill. Put self-sealing flat lids in a small saucepan, cover with water, bring to a boil, and boil for 5 minutes. Remove from the heat and let the lids stand in the water until needed. Have the ring bands ready.

2 Combine the bell peppers and chiles in a large nonreactive saucepan and add the sugar and vinegar. Place over high heat and bring to a boil, stirring to dissolve the sugar. Continue to boil for 3 minutes, stirring frequently. Remove the pan from the heat and let cool for 2 minutes. Add the liquid pectin and stir constantly for 2 minutes.

3 One at a time, remove the jars from the hot water, draining well, then ladle in the hot jelly mixture, filling to within ¼ inch (6 mm) of the rim. Wipe the rim clean of any drips, put the flat cap in place, and screw on the ring band. Let stand until cool, then check for a good seal; the lid should be concave. Let the jelly stand for 24 hours to set up before using. If the seal has not worked, store in the refrigerator for up to 3 weeks. If it has worked, store in a cool, dark place for up 1 year. You will need only a single jar of the jelly for this recipe; reserve the remainder for other uses.

4 To make the corn bread, pour the oil into a 9- or 10-inch (23- or 25-cm) cast-iron frying pan or other heavy ovenproof frying pan and place in a cold oven. Preheat the oven and pan to 450°F (230°C).

5 Meanwhile, in a large bowl, whisk together the cornmeal, flour, salt, baking powder, and baking soda. Make a well in the center. In another bowl, whisk together the eggs and the buttermilk until smooth.

6 When the oven reaches 450°F (230°C), add the egg mixture to the dry ingredients and stir gently just until blended. Remove the pan from the oven and swirl the oil to coat the bottom and sides of the pan. Pour the hot oil into the batter, whisking quickly to blend, and pour the batter into the hot pan.

7 Bake until the edges of the corn bread are crusty and brown and the surface is golden brown, about 15 minutes. (If you are not using a cast-iron pan, it could take 20–25 minutes.) Let cool in the pan for 5 minutes before slicing into wedges. Serve hot with the pepper jelly alongside.

DESSERTS AND SWEETS

Sugarcane, strawberries, pecans, and citrus are just a few of the

homegrown treats that contribute to the sweet life in Louisiana.

"Would you like a little something sweet?" This is a dangerous question in New Orleans, where the treat on offer could be a delicate praline, a refreshing scoop of Louisiana strawberry sorbet, or a slab of layer cake big enough for a dinner plate. Breakfast brings pecan waffles or calas (rice fritters) with sugarcane syrup. Sweltering afternoons call for spearmint snowballs, Sicilian fruit ices, or root beer floats. Restaurant dinners might end with a simple bread pudding or an all-out flaming finale such as bananas Foster. And a late night of bar hopping is best concluded over café au lait and beignets at Café du Monde.

LOUISIANA BLACKBERRY COBBLER WITH BLACKBERRY ICE CREAM

Whether you pluck them from the brambles or get stung by the shocking price at the supermarket, get 'em while you can: the season for Louisiana blackberries is short and sweet, spanning only a few weeks from mid-April through early May. This homey dessert makes the most out of that fleeting season, although both the ice cream and cobbler could also be made with frozen blackberries (or with fresh or frozen blueberries or raspberries). Don't be alarmed by the scanty amount of dough: rather than covering the fruit like a pie crust, it is scattered on top like cobblestones, hence the name of the dish.

1 To make the ice cream, in a small nonreactive saucepan over medium heat, lightly mash the berries with ½ cup (4 oz/125 g) of the sugar and the lemon juice, stirring until the berries are very juicy and the sugar is dissolved, 2–3 minutes. Remove from the heat and stir in the cream. Strain through a fine-mesh sieve into a bowl, pressing against the pulp with the back of a spoon; discard the contents of the sieve. Cover and refrigerate until well chilled, at least 3 hours and up to overnight.

2 Taste the chilled blackberry mixture and add up to ¼ cup (2 oz/60 g) additional sugar, if needed. (Remember that freezing will dull the flavor, so the mixture should seem especially sweet.) Pour the blackberry mixture into an ice-cream maker and freeze according to the manufacturer's instructions. Transfer the ice cream to a container with an airtight lid and place in the freezer until serving.

3 To make the cobbler, preheat the oven to 400°F (200°C). Generously butter an 8-inch (20-cm) square baking dish.

4 Place the blackberries in a large bowl. Combine the ½ cup sugar and the cornstarch in a fine-mesh sieve and sift over the berries. Toss the berries to coat evenly. Pour the filling into the prepared baking dish.

5 In a food processor, combine the flour, the remaining 2 tablespoons sugar, the salt, baking powder, and lemon zest. Process briefly to blend. Cut the butter into 6 pieces and distribute evenly over the flour. Pulse 12 times, or until the mixture resembles coarse meal with chunks of butter the size of small peas. Transfer the mixture to a bowl.

6 Using a spoon, stir the egg into the dough. Then drop the dough by tablespoonfuls onto the surface of the filling, spacing the dough evenly.

7 Bake until the crust is golden brown and the filling is bubbly, about 30 minutes. Transfer to a wire rack and let cool for at least 10 minutes.

8 Serve warm or at room temperature. Spoon the cobbler into deep dishes and top each serving with a scoop of blackberry ice cream.

Serve with an icy pitcher of lemonade, or go all out with blackberry kir royales (Champagne or dry sparkling wine with a splash of blackberry brandy).

FOR THE BLACKBERRY
ICE CREAM

**4 cups (1 lb/500 g) fresh or
thawed frozen blackberries**

**½–¾ cup (4–6 oz/125–185 g)
sugar**

1 teaspoon fresh lemon juice

**1½ cups (12 fl oz/375 ml) heavy
(double) cream**

FOR THE COBBLER

**6 cups (1½ lb/750 g) fresh
blackberries**

**½ cup (4 oz/125 g) plus
2 tablespoons sugar**

**2 tablespoons cornstarch
(cornflour)**

**¾ cup (4 oz/125 g) all-purpose
(plain) flour**

¼ teaspoon fine sea salt

½ teaspoon baking powder

½ teaspoon grated lemon zest

**6 tablespoons (3 oz/90 g) chilled
unsalted butter**

1 large egg, lightly beaten

Makes 6–8 servings

BURNT SUGAR CAKE

Louisiana leads the nation in sugar production, with more than half a million acres (two hundred thousand hectares) devoted to its cultivation. When the autumn harvest is over, cane fields are burned to clear the remaining stalks, and the air is filled with the aromas of smoke and the molasses brewing at the refineries. Some of the sugarcane will be sent to rum distilleries, while most will be granulated for daily use. This old-fashioned burnt sugar cake, with the nontraditional splash of sugarcane rum, captures the flavors of the season. The addition of ground pecans adds the flavor of another fall crop.

FOR THE BURNT SUGAR SYRUP

⅔ cup (5 oz/155 g) sugar

⅔ cup (5 fl oz/160 ml) boiling water

FOR THE CAKE

2 cups (10 oz/315 g) all-purpose (plain) flour

1 tablespoon baking powder

½ teaspoon fine sea salt

½ cup (2 oz/60 g) ground pecans

¼ cup (2 fl oz/60 ml) sugarcane rum

½ cup (4 oz/125 g) unsalted butter, at room temperature

1½ cups (12 oz/375 g) sugar

2 large egg yolks and 3 large egg whites, at room temperature

FOR THE FROSTING

2 large egg whites

¼ teaspoon fine sea salt

3 tablespoons sugar

½ cup (5 fl oz/160 ml) light corn syrup

Makes 12–16 servings

1 To make the burnt sugar syrup, in a small, heavy saucepan over medium-high heat, cook the sugar without stirring just until it begins to liquefy. Whisk until all of the sugar is dissolved and the syrup is dark brown, 3–5 minutes. Immediately add the boiling water. (Be careful of spatters.) Whisk until blended, then boil without stirring until the syrup is thick and reduced to ½ cup (4 fl oz/125 ml), 8–10 minutes. Pour the syrup into a heatproof glass measuring pitcher and set aside to cool.

2 To make the cake, preheat the oven to 350°F (180°C). Butter two 8-inch (20-cm) round pans, then dust with flour, tapping out the excess. In a bowl, sift together the flour, baking powder, and salt. Whisk in the ground pecans until well blended and set aside. In a small bowl, whisk together ¾ cup (6 fl oz/180 ml) water, ¼ cup (2 fl oz/60 ml) of the burnt sugar syrup, and the rum. Set aside.

3 In a mixing bowl, using an electric mixer on medium speed, cream the butter with 1¼ cups (10 oz/315 g) of the sugar until fluffy, about 2 minutes. Add the egg yolks one at a time, beating well after each addition. Beat in the flour mixture in 3 batches alternately with the burnt sugar mixture, beginning and ending with the flour mixture.

4 In a large clean bowl, using an electric mixer on high speed, beat the egg whites until frothy. Gradually sprinkle in the remaining ¼ cup (2 oz/60 g) sugar and continue beating until stiff, glossy peaks form. Using a rubber spatula, gently fold the egg whites into the cake batter just until no white streaks remain. Pour the batter into the prepared pans, dividing it evenly.

5 Bake the cake until a toothpick inserted into the center comes out clean and the center springs back when lightly touched with a fingertip, about 20 minutes. Transfer to a wire rack and let the cake layers cool in the pans for 10 minutes. Run a knife around the edges of the pan and invert the layers onto the racks. Let cool completely.

6 To make the frosting, in a large bowl, combine the egg whites and salt. Using an electric mixer on high speed, beat until frothy. Gradually sprinkle in the sugar and continue beating until soft peaks form. In a small saucepan over medium-high heat, combine the corn syrup and the remaining ¼ cup (2 fl oz/60 ml) burnt sugar syrup and bring to a boil. With the mixer on medium-high speed, carefully pour the hot syrup over the egg whites in a thin stream. Beat until stiff peaks form and the frosting has cooled to room temperature, about 15 minutes.

7 Place 1 cake layer, top side down, on a serving plate. Spoon one-third of the frosting onto the top and spread it evenly to the edges. Place the second layer, top side up, on top of the frosted layer. Spread the remaining frosting over the top and sides of the cake. Cut into wedges to serve.

Serve with a light and sweet Muscat or Orange Muscat.

MELON SHERBET

A wedge of juicy, ice-cold watermelon is the perfect summertime dessert down South, a carefree finale for a seafood boil or barbecue. This tangy sherbet is just a bit more trouble, but it preserves the fresh flavor and color of the melon, and the simple method can be used with other fruits as well. It begins with a sweet cooked meringue that adds extra body and a frothy texture to the finished sherbet. Make it with cantaloupe, honeydew, or watermelon, or whip up a batch of each to create a trio of pastel scoops.

1 In a small nonreactive saucepan over high heat, combine the sugar and water and bring to a boil, stirring until the sugar dissolves. Continue boiling, without stirring, until the syrup reaches 238°F (114°C) on a candy thermometer (the soft-ball stage). To test without a thermometer, scoop out several drops of the syrup with a clean wooden spoon, dip the spoon into a bowl of ice water, and press the drops between your fingertips. If they come together in a soft and supple ball, the syrup is ready.

2 Meanwhile, in a large bowl, using an electric mixer on medium-high speed, beat together the egg whites and salt just until stiff peaks form. With the mixer running, slowly pour the hot sugar syrup into the beaten egg whites. Continue beating until glossy and cool, about 5 minutes.

3 In a food processor or blender, process the melon until a smooth purée forms. You will need 2 cups (16 fl oz/500 ml) purée; reserve the remainder for another use. Transfer the purée to a bowl and stir in the lemon juice. Then, using a rubber spatula, gently fold in the meringue just until no white streaks remain.

4 Pour the melon mixture into an ice-cream maker and freeze according to the manufacturer's instructions. Serve at once.

Serve with a dry Champagne.

1 cup (8 oz/250 g) sugar

¼ cup (2 fl oz/60 ml) water

2 large egg whites

Pinch of sea salt

3–4 cups (18–24 oz/560–750 g) peeled, seeded, and cubed cantaloupe, honeydew, or watermelon, well chilled

2 tablespoons fresh lemon juice

Makes about 1 qt (1 l)

Red to the Rind

"Watermelon—chief of the world's luxuries, king by the grace of God over all the fruits of the earth," Mark Twain said. "The true Southern watermelon is a boon apart, and not to be mentioned with commoner things.... It was not a Southern watermelon that Eve took; we know it because she repented."

The massive gourd has been around since biblical times and was probably born in the Kalahari Desert. It appeared in Egyptian cave paintings and tombs over four thousand years ago and was a favorite in China by the tenth century. Introduced to southern Europe by the Moors in the thirteenth century, the watermelon traveled to North America with European colonists and African slaves.

The first American cookbook, *American Cookery* by Ameila Simmons (1796), contained a recipe for pickled watermelon rind. Thomas Jefferson boasted that the melons at Monticello were sweeter than those in Paris, and confederate soldiers boiled down the juice to use as a sugar substitute. How do you pick a good one? Thump it and listen for the echo, which signals a ripe, juicy melon.

CARNIVAL KING CAKE

Cakes honoring the Magi are served on Epiphany (January 6) in many Catholic cultures, including France and Mexico. In Louisiana, however, they herald the arrival of the dozens of kings and queens who will reign over various Carnival balls and parades. The decorated brioche rings are a New Orleans specialty seen in bakeries and supermarkets in the weeks leading up to Mardi Gras, from Twelfth Night until Ash Wednesday. If you "get the baby" (a small plastic trinket concealed in one of the slices), you must provide the cake for the next party.

⅓ cup (3 oz/90 g) sugar

Grated zest of 1 lemon

4 cups (1¼ lb/625 g) all-purpose (plain) flour

1 teaspoon fine sea salt

1 package (2½ teaspoons) active dry yeast

¾ cup (6 oz/185 g) chilled unsalted butter

3 large eggs

1 cup (8 fl oz/250 ml) whole milk

1 ovenproof charm, such as a Mardi Gras baby, or a whole almond

1 large egg yolk whisked with 1 tablespoon water, for brushing

Purple, green, and gold (yellow) decorating sugars

Makes 16 servings

1 In a food processor, combine the sugar and lemon zest and process for 15 seconds to blend. Add the flour, salt, and yeast and process for another 15 seconds to blend. Cut the butter into 12 pieces and distribute the pieces evenly around the processor bowl, pushing them down into the flour mixture. Pulse about 15 times, or until the mixture resembles coarse meal.

2 In a large measuring pitcher or a bowl with a spout, whisk together the eggs and milk. With the processor running, pour the egg mixture through the feed tube and process for 30–40 seconds, stopping to scrape down the sides if necessary. The dough should be very soft and sticky.

3 Scrape the dough into a large bowl, cover tightly, and refrigerate overnight. It will stiffen as it chills to the consistency of a dense cookie dough.

4 Line a baking sheet with parchment (baking) paper. Working quickly, before the dough warms up and begins to soften, place the cold dough on the parchment and use your hand to mold it into an oblong ring about 12 inches (30 cm) long and 2 inches (5 cm) wide with a hole in the center. Using

damp hands, pat the ring smooth. Push the charm or the almond into the underside of the dough to conceal it. Cover the dough ring loosely with another sheet of parchment paper. Set the pan aside in a warm, draft-free place and let the dough rise until doubled in size, about 3 hours.

5 Preheat the oven to 375°F (190°C). Brush the surface of the dough gently and evenly with the egg yolk mixture. Sprinkle generously with the decorating sugars, alternating wide stripes of purple, green, and gold.

6 Bake until golden brown, 25–30 minutes. Transfer to a wire rack and let the cake cool on the pan for at least 10 minutes.

7 Transfer the cake to a serving plate and serve warm or at room temperature. Cut on the diagonal into thin slices.

Toast the Carnival season (and the guest who gets the baby) with demi-sec Champagne.

BOURBON PECAN TART

Broad, leafy pecan trees grew wild along the bayous of Louisiana for centuries before they were cultivated commercially, and the trees are still prized by homeowners for the cool shade they provide in summer and the bountiful harvests they produce in fall. Gooey and sticky sweet, pecan pie is the quintessential Southern dessert. Here, it is transformed into a buttery tart that requires less sugar than the original but preserves the crisp top layer of nuts. A shot of bourbon is added for good measure.

1 To make the pastry, in a food processor, combine the flour and salt and pulse briefly to blend. Cut the butter into 8 pieces and distribute the pieces evenly over the flour. Pulse 10 times, or until the mixture resembles coarse meal. Sprinkle the ice water over the surface and pulse 7 more times. The dough will appear rather loose but should hold together when pressed between your fingers. Shape the dough into a disk ¾ inch (2 cm) thick, wrap tightly in plastic wrap, and refrigerate for at least 30 minutes or up to overnight.

2 Preheat the oven to 350°F (180°C). On a lightly floured work surface, roll out the dough into a round 12 inches (30 cm) in diameter and ⅛ inch (3 mm) thick. Roll the round loosely around the pin, then carefully unroll it over the top of a 9-inch (23-cm) tart pan with a removable bottom, allowing the excess to drape over the sides. Press the pastry gently into the bottom and sides of the pan, then roll the pin across the top of the pan, trimming off the excess dough.

3 To make the filling, in a bowl, using an electric mixer on medium speed, beat together the eggs, sugar, salt, and cinnamon until smooth. Add the molasses, butter, and bourbon and beat until thoroughly combined. Stir in the pecans. Pour the filling into the prepared tart shell.

4 Bake until a knife inserted near the center comes out clean, 45–50 minutes. Transfer to a wire rack, let cool for 10 minutes, then remove the pan sides and let cool completely. Carefully slide the tart off the pan bottom onto a serving plate.

FOR THE PASTRY

1½ cups (7½ oz/235 g) all-purpose (plain) flour

½ teaspoon fine sea salt

½ cup (4 oz/125 g) chilled unsalted butter

3 tablespoons ice water

FOR THE FILLING

2 large eggs

½ cup (4 oz/125 g) sugar

¼ teaspoon fine sea salt

¼ teaspoon ground cinnamon

⅔ cup (7½ oz/235 g) molasses

2 tablespoons unsalted butter, melted

2 tablespoons good-quality bourbon

1¼ cups (7 oz/220 g) pecan halves

Makes 8 servings

The Bourbon Connection

Kentucky's Bourbon County, like Bourbon Street in New Orleans, was named in honor of the French royal house, but it has since become better known for its liquor. According to legend, America's native whiskey owes its amber hue and smooth flavor to the thrift of Reverend Elijah Craig, who singed oak barrels to burn away any contaminants and then shipped his spirits in them to the port of New Orleans. The barrels were stamped with the name of his Kentucky county and filled with a clear corn distillate, which was mellowed and colored by the oak during its journey down the Mississippi.

The traditional character of bourbon is protected by a congressional resolution, passed in 1964, that established strict guidelines for its production. Among other requirements, bourbon must be made from a mash that contains at least 51 percent corn, and it must age in new barrels made from charred white oak.

In addition to mint juleps and holiday eggnog, residents of Louisiana use bourbon to spike pecan pies, fruitcakes, candied yams, and even barbecue sauce.

CALAS

"Calas! Hot and sweet!" was once a familiar cry in the French Quarter, where singing vendors strolled with their baskets until the 1940s. According to legend, many slaves earned the money to buy their freedom by selling the fragrant rice fritters. Calas can be rolled in cinnamon sugar, as they are here, dusted with confectioners' (icing) sugar, or drizzled with cane syrup. They are great for a special brunch or a lazy weekend breakfast, because the yeasted rice mixture can be left to rise overnight to yield a particularly light version of these small ethereal puffs.

1½ cups (7½ oz/235 g) uncooked long-grain white rice

1 package (2½ teaspoons) active dry yeast

3 large eggs, at room temperature

½ teaspoon finely grated lemon zest

½ teaspoon vanilla extract (essence)

1¼ cups (5 oz/155 g) sifted all-purpose (plain) flour

¼ cup (2 oz/60 g) sugar

½ teaspoon fine sea salt

½ teaspoon ground cinnamon

½ teaspoon freshly grated nutmeg

Vegetable oil for deep frying

1 cup (8 oz/250 g) sugar mixed with 2 tablespoons ground cinnamon

Cane syrup for serving (optional)

Makes about 24 fritters

1 In a small saucepan over medium-high heat, bring the rice and 1 cup (8 fl oz/250 ml) water to a boil. Reduce the heat to low, cover the pan tightly, and steam until all of the water is absorbed and the rice is very soft, about 30 minutes.

2 In a bowl, using a fork, mash the rice until it forms a coarse paste. Set aside to cool until the rice is lukewarm. In a small bowl, sprinkle the yeast over ½ cup (4 fl oz/125 ml) warm water (110°F/43°C) and let stand until creamy, about 5 minutes. Pour the yeast mixture into the lukewarm rice and stir to blend well. Cover the bowl tightly with plastic wrap and leave in a warm spot for several hours or up to overnight.

3 In a separate bowl, whisk together the eggs, lemon zest, and vanilla until blended. Combine the flour, sugar, salt, cinnamon, and nutmeg in a sifter or fine-mesh sieve and sift over the rice mixture. Add the egg mixture to the rice mixture and stir gently just until all the ingredients are combined. Cover and set aside in a warm place until the dough is light and spongy, about 30 minutes.

4 Preheat the oven to 200°F (95°C). Pour oil to a depth of 3 inches (7.5 cm) into a deep, heavy saucepan or a deep fryer and heat to 350°F (180°C) on a deep-frying thermometer. Line a platter with several layers of paper towels and set it near the stove.

5 Working in batches, drop the dough by large tablespoonfuls into the hot oil, being careful not to crowd the pan. Fry until golden brown, about 3 minutes. The calas should turn over by themselves as they cook; if they don't, give them a gentle push with a long-handled fork or a chopstick. Using a slotted spoon or a wire skimmer, transfer the calas to the paper towels to drain. Keep warm in the oven until all the fritters are fried.

6 Spread the cinnamon sugar in a shallow bowl. One or two at a time, roll the hot fritters in the cinnamon sugar and arrange on a warmed platter. Serve at once, with the cane syrup if desired.

For a true Creole breakfast, serve with dark French-drip coffee, with or without hot milk.

STRAWBERRY SHORTCAKE

A marriage made in heaven, strawberries and cream are the perfect couple. Here they are heaped between the two halves of a warm shortcake, a big buttery biscuit that's crisp around the edges, fluffy in the middle, and split to soak up plenty of the sweet red juice. Accompanied by an icy pitcher of lemonade, this old-fashioned dessert would be right at home on a big screened porch in Ponchatoula, strawberry capital of Louisiana and home to the annual strawberry festival. This historic farm town, just northwest of New Orleans, is also famous for its country antiques shops and auctions.

1 Preheat the oven to 375°F (190°C). Butter an 8- or 9-inch (20- or 23-cm) round cake pan with 1 tablespoon of the room temperature butter.

2 In a food processor, combine the flour, the ½ cup sugar, the baking powder, salt, and baking soda. Process briefly to blend. Cut the ½ cup chilled butter into 8 pieces and distribute the pieces evenly around the processor bowl. Pulse 8–10 times, or until the mixture resembles coarse meal with chunks of butter the size of small peas. Turn the mixture into a bowl and form a well in the center.

3 In a separate bowl, using a balloon whisk, beat the eggs just until blended, then beat in the buttermilk until smooth. Add the egg mixture to the well in the dry ingredients and stir gently just until blended. Scrape the dough into the prepared pan and smooth the top.

4 Bake until the top is golden brown and springy to the touch, about 25 minutes. Transfer to a wire rack and let cool in the pan for about 10 minutes.

5 While the cake is baking, using a paring knife, hull and halve the strawberries. In a bowl, toss the strawberries with the remaining ⅓ cup sugar. Set aside for at least 30 minutes, tossing occasionally, to release the strawberry juices.

6 While the cake is cooling, in a bowl, using an electric mixer on medium-high speed, beat the cream just until soft peaks form.

7 Turn the warm shortcake out onto a large flat serving plate, then carefully turn it upright. Using a long serrated knife, cut the cake in half horizontally, creating 2 layers. Carefully slide the top half onto another plate. Spread the cut surface of the bottom half with the remaining 2 tablespoons butter. Spoon the juice from the berries onto the bottom layer, allowing it to soak in, then pile on the berries followed by the whipped cream. Replace the top half of the cake and serve at once, in wedges, while still warm.

Serve with a sweet Riesling or demi-sec Champagne.

3 tablespoons unsalted butter, at room temperature, plus ½ cup (4 oz/125 g) chilled

2 cups (10 oz/315 g) all-purpose (plain) flour

½ cup (4 oz/125 g) plus ⅓ cup (3 oz/90 g) sugar

2 teaspoons baking powder

½ teaspoon fine sea salt

¼ teaspoon baking soda (bicarbonate of soda)

2 large eggs, at room temperature

¾ cup (6 fl oz/180 ml) buttermilk

4 cups (1 lb/500 g) strawberries

1 cup (8 fl oz/250 ml) heavy (double) cream

Makes 6–8 servings

CAFÉ BRÛLOT CUSTARD

At old-style Creole restaurants, the lights are dimmed as a waiter rolls out a tableside cart topped with a chafing dish of strong coffee. The waiter spices it with cloves, cinnamon sticks, and lemon peel; adds warm brandy; and then sets it alight, stirring the flaming brew with much ceremony and flourish before ladling it into cups. Café brûlot is usually a grand finale for a rich and very expensive meal. It inspired this simple dessert that re-creates the same flavors in a homey custard. Using half-and-half yields an especially luxurious dessert, but it's also fine to substitute whole milk.

1¼ cups (10 oz/310 g) sugar

2 cups (16 fl oz/500 ml) half-and-half (half cream)

2 teaspoons instant espresso powder

4 large eggs

2 tablespoons brandy

1 teaspoon grated lemon zest

½ teaspoon ground cinnamon

¼ teaspoon ground cloves

⅛ teaspoon fine sea salt

Makes 8 servings

1 Preheat the oven to 325°F (165°C). In a small, heavy saucepan over medium-high heat, cook ¾ cup (6 oz/185 g) of the sugar without stirring just until it begins to liquefy. Reduce the heat to low and whisk until the sugar dissolves and the syrup is amber, 2–4 minutes.

2 Immediately pour the syrup into eight ½-cup (4–fl oz/125-ml) individual custard cups or a 4-cup (32–fl oz/1-l) flan dish or shallow round baking dish. Working quickly, swirl each cup or the dish to coat the bottom and sides. (The syrup will harden almost immediately but return to a syrup-like consistency after the custard bakes and chills.)

3 In a small, heavy saucepan over medium heat, warm the half-and-half just until bubbles appear along the edges of the pan. Stir in the espresso powder, remove from the heat, and let cool slightly.

4 Heat a kettle full of water on the stove top until very hot but not boiling. In a bowl, whisk the eggs with the remaining ½ cup (4 oz/125 g) sugar, the brandy, lemon zest, cinnamon, cloves, and salt until blended. Continue whisking as you drizzle in the hot coffee mixture.

5 Place the caramel-lined cups or dish in a large baking pan. Pour the custard through a fine-mesh sieve into the cups, dividing it evenly, or into the dish. Pour the hot water into the baking pan to reach halfway up the sides of the cups or the dish.

6 Bake until the custard is set in the center when it is gently shaken, 50–60 minutes. Carefully transfer the cups or dish from the hot water to a wire rack and let cool to room temperature. Cover and refrigerate until well chilled, at least 4 hours or up to 2 days.

7 Loosen the edges of the chilled custard with a thin knife blade. If using custard cups, invert a small dessert plate over each cup and, holding the plate and cup, invert them together. Lift off the cup, holding it over the custard until all of the caramel has released from the cup. If using a large dish, invert a large round serving plate over the custard and follow the same instructions above. Cut the large custard into wedges before serving. Serve chilled.

Serve with small cups of espresso garnished with a twist of shaved lemon rind.

BEIGNETS

No trip to New Orleans is complete without hot beignets, pillow-shaped crullers dusted with confectioners' sugar. They were originally served as a dawn meal for dockworkers and merchants at the old French Market. The eggy yeast dough is rolled into very thin pieces and tossed into hot fat before it rises, so it balloons in the pan, yielding a crisp brown crust and airy center. To make café au lait, the traditional accompaniment, brew strong chicory coffee and heat milk in a pan, then pour equal measures of both into a large cup.

1 In a small bowl, sprinkle the yeast over the warm water and let stand until creamy, about 5 minutes. In a food processor, combine 3 cups (15 oz/470 g) of the flour, the granulated sugar, and salt. Process briefly.

2 In a small saucepan over medium heat, combine the milk and butter and heat gently until the milk is warm but not steaming and the butter melts. Remove from the heat. With the processor running, pour the milk mixture through the feed tube and process until blended. Add the egg, yeast mixture, and the remaining 1½ cups (7½ oz/235 g) flour and process just until a soft dough forms.

3 Preheat the oven to 200°F (95°C). Line an ovenproof platter with paper towels. Pour oil to a depth of 3 inches (7.5 cm) into a deep, heavy saucepan or a deep fryer and heat to 360°F (182°C) on a deep-frying thermometer.

4 While the oil is heating, divide the dough into 2 equal pieces. On a well-floured work surface, knead 1 piece of the dough briefly until soft but not sticky. Roll into a rectangle about ¼ inch (6 mm) thick. Cut into 6 equal rectangles. When the oil is ready, drop 2 or 3 rectangles into the oil and fry, turning once, until puffed and brown, about 2 minutes on each side. Transfer to the paper towels and keep warm in the oven. Repeat with the remaining rectangles, and then the remaining dough. Arrange on a warmed plate and, using a fine-mesh sieve, dust the calas heavily with confectioners' sugar. Serve at once.

Serve with steaming cups of café au lait.

1 package (2½ teaspoons) active dry yeast

¼ cup (2 fl oz/60 ml) cup warm (110°F/43°C) water

4½ cups (22½ oz/705 g) all-purpose (plain) flour

3 tablespoons granulated sugar

¾ teaspoon fine sea salt

1 cup (8 fl oz/250 ml) whole milk

4 tablespoons (2 oz/60 g) unsalted butter

1 large egg

Peanut or canola oil for deep-frying

Confectioners' (icing) sugar for dusting

Makes about 12 beignets

Coffee Culture

More than two hundred years ago, Exchange Alley in the French Quarter was lined with coffeehouses (then known as "exchanges"), meeting spots where merchants and financiers indulged in the dark brew as they traded news on the burgeoning colony. By the mid-nineteenth century, New Orleans was home to some five hundred coffeehouses. It was also the main point of entry for coffee from the Caribbean and South America.

Locals prefer a dark French roast, either taken pure or drunk in the New Orleans blend of coffee and chicory. The roasted and ground chicory root, originally used to extend scarce coffee beans during wartime, is now favored for the extra body and aroma it contributes. Louisiana's best-known coffee brands are CDM and Community.

CDM is named for the venerable Café du Monde, an essential stop for café au lait and beignets overlooking Jackson Square. Crowded with tourists and locals, well-dressed revelers and street people, it has been open around the clock since the 1860s, closing only for Christmas and the occasional hurricane.

LEMON ICEBOX PIE

Sweetened condensed milk is a common ingredient in Deep South desserts. A convenience in the days before refrigeration, it's now used as a matter of taste, as in this wonderfully refreshing and lemony icebox pie. The flavor is intensified by adding grated lemon zest to both the graham cracker crust and whipped cream topping. In many traditional recipes, the filling contains raw egg yolks, which are thickened to a custardlike consistency through a chemical reaction with the acidic juice. Here, however, the pie is baked just long enough to cook the yolks while retaining its fresh flavor.

FOR THE CRUST

1 cup (3 oz/90 g) graham cracker crumbs

½ cup (2 oz/60 g) coarsely ground pecans

2 tablespoons sugar

2 teaspoons grated lemon zest

4 tablespoons (2 oz/60 g) unsalted butter, melted

FOR THE FILLING

4 large egg yolks

1 tablespoon grated lemon zest

1 can (14 fl oz/440 ml) sweetened condensed milk

½ cup (4 fl oz/125 ml) fresh lemon juice, strained

FOR THE TOPPING

1 cup (8 fl oz/250 ml) heavy (double) cream

1 tablespoon sugar, or more to taste

½ teaspoon grated lemon zest

Makes 6–8 servings

1 To, make the crust, preheat the oven to 300°F (150°C). In a bowl, toss together the graham cracker crumbs, pecans, sugar, and lemon zest. Stir in the melted butter until well blended.

2 Transfer the crumb mixture to an 8- or 9-inch (20- or 23-cm) pie dish or pan and, using your fingers, press it firmly and evenly into the bottom and up the sides. Bake until set, about 10 minutes. Transfer to a wire rack and let cool completely. Raise the oven temperature to 325°F (165°C).

3 While the crust is cooling, make the filling. In a bowl, use an electric mixer to beat together the egg yolks with lemon zest until very light and frothy, about 2 minutes. Add the sweetened condensed milk, beat until smooth, and then stir in the lemon juice. Set aside until slightly thickened, about 15 minutes.

4 Pour the filling into the cooled crust. Bake until the filling is softly set, about 15 minutes. Transfer to a wire rack and let cool to room temperature. Cover and refrigerate for at least 4 hours or up to 2 days.

5 Just before serving, make the topping: In a bowl, using an electric mixer on medium speed, whip the cream until very frothy. Sprinkle with the sugar and lemon zest and continue whipping until soft peaks form.

6 Spread the whipped cream evenly over the top of the chilled pie. Cut into wedges to serve.

Serve with a rich Sauternes to complement the cool and creamy citrus flavors of the pie.

GLOSSARY

BELL PEPPERS Sweet-fleshed, bell-shaped members of the pepper family, bell peppers are also known as sweet peppers or capsicums. Green bell peppers are usually more sharply flavored than red ones, the latter being simply a sweeter and more mature stage of the former. Orange and yellow bell peppers are separate varieties. To core and seed a bell pepper, cut the pepper in half lengthwise and remove the stem and seeds with your fingers. Trim away the remaining white membranes, or ribs, brush or rinse away any remaining seeds, and cut to the desired size and shape.

BIBB LETTUCE Also called limestone, Bibb lettuce has pale green leaves loosely gathered in a small, rosettelike head. Part of the butterhead family, Bibb lettuce is sweet and has tender leaves. Store unwashed in a plastic bag in the refrigerator.

BREAD CRUMBS Bread crumbs, fresh or dry, are the good cook's secret weapon, bestowing a crisp topping on casseroles and a crunchy coating on pan-fried meats. About 2 ounces (60 g) of bread, or one slice, makes $\frac{1}{2}$ cup of bread crumbs.

TO MAKE DRY BREAD CRUMBS, dry out slices of day-old French or other good-quality white bread in a 200°F (95°C) oven for about 1 hour. Break the bread into bite-sized pieces and process in a blender or food processor to the desired consistency. Dried bread crumbs will keep for up to 1 month in the refrigerator.

TO MAKE FRESH BREAD CRUMBS, trim the crusts from slices of day-old bread. Baguettes, Italian- or French-style bread, whole-wheat (wholemeal) breads, and egg breads make good crumbs. Tear the bread into large pieces, put in a food processor, and process to the desired consistency.

BROWN SUGAR Rich in flavor, brown sugar is granulated sugar colored with molasses. It has a soft, moist texture and comes in mild-flavored light brown and stronger-flavored dark brown varieties.

CAYENNE PEPPER A very hot ground red pepper made from dried cayenne and other chiles, cayenne is used sparingly to add heat or to heighten the flavors of a dish. Because different blends vary in heat, always begin with a very small amount and add more to taste in small pinches.

CHILES Over centuries of domestication, hundreds of chile varieties have been developed. Requiring hot summers, they grow well in tropical areas and can be large or tiny, mild or fiery, sprinkled as a season-ing or cooked as a vegetable. To reduce the heat of fresh chiles, carefully cut out the ribs, or membranes, and discard the seeds. When working with any fresh chiles, avoid touching your eyes, mouth, or other sensitive areas. You may also wish to use rubber gloves to protect your skin.

JALAPEÑO This bright-green, broad-shouldered chile, about $1\frac{1}{2}$ inches (4 cm) long, ranges from hot to very hot and is one of the most widely used in the United States. It is available canned or fresh and is sometimes seen in its bright red-ripe state.

SERRANO A slender, shiny red or green chile about 3 inches (7.5 cm) long and very hot.

CONDENSED MILK Condensed milk is evaporated milk with a high proportion (40 percent) of cane sugar. Also known as sweetened condensed milk, condensed milk was developed in 1856 as a way of preserving whole milk without refrigeration. It is ivory in color and has a syrupy consistency and glossy surface. Sold in cans, condensed milk is used most often in confections and desserts. It will thicken when combined with acidic fruit juice. Do not substitute evaporated milk.

CORN SYRUP Made from cornstarch (cornflour), corn syrup is used to sweeten everything from candies and jams to homemade pie and tart fillings. Dark corn syrup has more flavor than light syrup; the two are not generally interchangeable in recipes.

DUCK, MUSCOVY The leanest domestic duck, Muscovy ducks reach the market slightly older than other ducks, nearly 3 months old, which results in especially full-flavored breast meat. Breasts may be marketed as magrets. Muscovies are also raised for excellent foie gras. Look for it in well-stocked meat markets or online through reputable food vendors.

FILÉ *See sassafras.*

GIZZARD Part of a fowl's intestinal system, the gizzard grinds the bird's food, often with the help of swallowed stones or grit. The center of the gizzard is usually removed before the fowl is sold. Cook slowly with moist heat to avoid toughness.

GOAT CHEESE Cheese made from goat's milk. The French term is *fromage de chèvre,* which is often shortened to *chèvre.* Look for it in specialty stores and well-stocked supermarkets.

GRANA PADANO Similar to Parmigiano-Reggiano, *grana padano* is produced north of the river Po and is matured for less time than Parmesan cheese, resulting in a slightly milder taste. As it is not held to the same production and aging standards as Parmigiano-Reggiano, it is often less expensive.

GREENS Hearty in flavor and high in nutrients, dark greens, also known as cooking greens, come from many different vegetable families and range in flavor from lemony to peppery. Look for fresh, crisp leaves free of blemishes or yellow spots when buy-ing. Small, tender young leaves have a milder flavor than more mature greens and can be used raw in salads or on sandwiches. Available year-round, but most are best in late winter or early spring.

COLLARD GREENS This favorite in the American South has large, thick, dark green leaves and a mild flavor. Because of their tough texture, they are typically cooked for a longer time than other greens.

DANDELION GREENS The pale green sawtooth leaves of the dandelion have a pleasantly bitter fla-vor. Cultivated dandelion greens are more tender than wild, which should not be eaten unless you are certain they haven't been sprayed with chemicals.

ESCAROLE A slightly bitter member of the chicory family with broad, ruffled leaves.

KALE A member of the cabbage family, with firm, tightly crinkled leaves on a long stem, kale has a dark green color and an earthy flavor. It holds its texture well when cooked.

MUSTARD GREENS Light green with hints of yellow, mustard greens come in varying sizes and shapes. Those with large leaves tend to be sweeter than those loosely formed into heads. Mustard greens with small, curled leaves have the spiciest flavor.

SWISS CHARD Also known simply as chard, it has crinkled leaves on fleshy, ribbed stems that are either red or white. Red chard has an earthy flavor, while white is a bit sweeter.

GRITS In the South, grits—from the Middle English *gyrt,* meaning bran—refers specifically to hominy grits, coarsely ground from the dried kernels of hulled mature white corn. Grits are available in several forms: stone-ground grits, which take about 40 minutes to cook; regular coarse-grained grits, which take about 20 minutes to cook; quick-cooking grits, which have a finer texture and cook in about 5 minutes; and instant grits, which have been pre-cooked and dried (the latter sacrifice some flavor and texture for the sake of speed). All over the South grits are served with eggs and cured meats at breakfast, and also as a side dish with lunch or dinner.

HORSERADISH This gnarled root has a pungent flavor that contributes a spicy bite to sauces and side dishes. Look for fresh horseradish in produce markets, or use bottled, or prepared, horseradish, which is grated and mixed with vinegar.

LIQUID PECTIN Pectin, a flavorless, gelatin-like substance found naturally in fruits, is valued for its ability to "set" or jell jams, jellies, and preserves. You can find it in both liquid and powdered forms in major supermarkets. Store in an airtight container away from light and moisture.

MIRLITONS These native North American pale green gourds with a nondescript flavor are similar to cucumbers or zucchini (courgettes) and have been a regional staple since prehistoric times. Prolific to the point of nuisance, mirlitons, known as chayotes in the Southwest and christophenes in the Caribbean, are commonly cultivated by New Orleans gardeners, who use them in slaw, pickles, casseroles, and cakes. The sturdy shell takes well to stuffing, forming a plump boat for the traditional dressing of butter-sautéed seasonings, bread crumbs, and shrimp.

MOLASSES A thick, robust-tasting syrup, molasses is a by-product of cane sugar refining. Light molasses is mixed with pure cane syrup and has the lightest flavor and color. Dark molasses is thicker, darker, stronger in flavor, and less sweet than light molasses. Both light and dark molasses may be bleached with sulfur dioxide. Processed without sulfur, unsulfured molasses has a milder flavor. Molasses gives a distinctive flavor to many sweet and savory baked foods.

OKRA This homely pod can be slimy, and many varieties are a bit fuzzy, but stew it with tomatoes and shrimp or fry it in a crisp coating of cornmeal and all is forgiven. Okra was probably introduced to the Americas by African slaves, who carried the seeds from their homeland. Known in the Bantu language as *gumbo,* it thickens and flavors the famous Southern soup of the same name. Hot pickled okra, available commercially packed in jars, makes a startling garnish for Bloody Marys, Louisiana style.

ONIONS, SWEET VIDALIA Pale yellow Vidalia onions are named for their place of origin in the state of Georgia. They are prized for their sweet and mild flavor.

PECAN OIL Made from pecans, pecan oil has a rich flavor and is used as a seasoning or blended into dressings and sauces. Like all nut oils, it turns rancid quickly, so use it within 3 months of purchase.

PECANS Native to North America, the pecan has two deeply crinkled lobes of nutmeat, much like its relative the walnut. The nuts have smooth, brown oval shells that break easily. Their flavor is sweeter and more delicate than that of walnuts.

TO MAKE TOASTED SPICY-SWEET PECANS, preheat the oven to 325°F (165°C). In a small bowl, toss ½ cup (2 oz/60 g) pecan halves or pieces with 1 tablespoon unsalted butter, melted; 2 tablespoons sugar; ½ teaspoon salt; and ¼ teaspoon cayenne pepper until evenly coated. Spread in a single layer on a small rimmed baking sheet and bake until lightly toasted, about 10 minutes. These spicy nuts can be used to garnish salads, meats, vegetables, and desserts, or they can be eaten out of hand.

QUAIL Two of the most popular game birds for cooking are quail and squab. Quail are quite tiny, weighing about ½ pound (250 g) each. They are sometimes sold partially deboned, with the breastbones removed, making them easier to prepare.

RED CHILE PASTE A very hot condiment made of chopped or ground chiles and (usually) vinegar and salt, used extensively in Southeast Asia, China, and Korea. Do not confuse with American "chile sauce."

ROUX A mixture of flour and a fat such as butter or oil, roux is a common thickening agent in sauces and gravies. Roux is made by stirring flour into hot oil or butter and stirring the mixture over the heat for a few minutes, or sometimes longer, to eliminate the raw taste of the flour. Roux can be white, blond, or brown. White and blond roux are made with butter and used to thicken cream sauces and soups, while brown roux is made with oil or animal fat. Brown roux has a rich, nutty flavor that is an essential part of many Creole dishes, such as gumbo.

SASSAFRAS Also known as gumbo filé, this olive-green powder is made from the dried, pulverized leaves of the sassafras plant and is prized by the Cajuns of Louisiana for its thickening abilities. Its name comes from the French verb *filer,* which means "to spin threads," and, true to its name, filé can get stringy if cooked too long. To avoid this, add it just a few minutes before serving. Look for it in the spice aisle of well-stocked supermarkets, or try a specialty market that carries Southern food products.

SATSUMAS A small Japanese mandarin orange that is almost seedless and easy to peel. Most canned mandarin oranges are satsumas. Look for them in most supermarkets in late fall and winter.

SHIITAKE MUSHROOMS The most popular mushrooms in Japan are now widely cultivated. Buff to dark brown in appearance, they are widely available fresh and dried. Remove their thin, tough stems before using.

SUGARCANE RUM A spirit that originated in the Caribbean, rum is distilled from sugarcane juice or molasses. This slightly sweet liquor is especially well suited for mixed drinks and desserts. The darker the rum, the stronger its flavor. As for other spirits, the alcohol content of rum is designated by its proof, which is always twice the percentage of alcohol (80-proof rum, for example, is 40 percent alcohol).

SWEET POTATOES Native to North America, sweet potatoes are either yellow-brown with yellow flesh, or dark reddish or purplish with dark orange flesh. The latter variety is commonly known in the United

States as a yam, although it is a different species from the true yam. Although available year-round, their actual season is fall and winter. Choose firm, unblemished sweet potatoes without any breaks in the thin skin.

TEMPURA BATTER Cooks in New Orleans like to deep-fry nearly every kind of food. This light batter is particularly well suited to small birds, such as quail, and to myriad vegetables.

TO MAKE TEMPURA BATTER, in a bowl, stir together ¼ cup (1½ oz/45 g) all-purpose (plain) flour, ¼ cup (1 oz/ 30 g) cornstarch (cornflour), and ½ cup (4 fl oz/125 ml) water; the batter should have the consistency of heavy (double) cream. If it is too thick, add a splash of club soda. Season with salt and freshly ground pepper, then use at once.

THAI FISH SAUCE Southeast Asians use fish sauce in the same way that Westerners use salt, both as a cooking seasoning and at the table. Made from salted and fermented fish, it is a thin, clear liquid that ranges in color from amber to dark brown. Famous for its pungent aroma and strong, salty flavor, it is often mixed with other ingredients and used as a dipping sauce.

TOMATOES Tomatoes are generally available in three types: round, plum, and cherry. Medium- or large-sized round tomatoes are excellent for slicing, while egg-shaped plum, or Roma, varieties have more pulp and less juice, making them perfect for sauces. Small cherry tomatoes are available in a variety of colors and shapes.

TO PEEL AND SEED TOMATOES, cut a shallow X in the blossom end of the tomato. Immerse in a pan of boiling water until the peel begins to curl away from the X, about 30 seconds. Transfer to a bowl of ice water to cool, then peel away the skin. To seed, cut in half crosswise and squeeze each half gently to dislodge the seeds.

TO MAKE FRESH TOMATO PURÉE, peel and seed the tomatoes as above. Purée until smooth in a blender or a food processor.

TROUT A freshwater fish with wonderfully sweet, white flesh, trout is widely available whole, boned, or in fillets. Trout can be fried, grilled, broiled, or braised. Look also for pink-fleshed trout.

TRUFFLE OIL Olive oil infused with the aroma of truffles, an aromatic fungus found in Italy and France. White truffles are usually used to make truffle oil. Available in specialty stores.

VINEGAR Made from fermented liquids, such as red or white wine, beer, or cider, vinegar has been used for centuries throughout the world. Store in a cool, dry cupboard.

CANE VINEGAR Made from sugarcane, cane vinegar is rich with a slightly sweet flavor. Available in specialty stores.

CHAMPAGNE VINEGAR Made from fermented Champagne grapes, Champagne vinegar has a light, sweet taste. Available in specialty stores.

CIDER VINEGAR Made from apples, cider vinegar is commonly used in many traditional American recipes and is noted for its distinctive apple flavor. For the best flavor, buy real cider vinegar, not cider-flavored distilled vinegar.

RICE WINE VINEGAR Made from fermented rice and widely used in Asian cuisines. It is used to add a slight acidity in cooked dishes and to make dressings for delicate greens. Rice wine vinegar is available either plain or sweetened.

TARRAGON VINEGAR Tarragon vinegar is simply white vinegar that has been flavored with tarragon. You can find it in most well-stocked supermarkets.

WORCESTERSHIRE SAUCE A traditional English condiment, Worcestershire sauce is an intensely flavorful and savory blend of molasses, soy sauce, garlic, onion, anchovies, and other ingredients. Often used in marinades for grilled food, it can also be passed at the table.

INGREDIENT SOURCES

CAFÉ DU MONDE
Coffee and chickory, French roast coffee, and beignet mix
(800) 772-2927
shop.cafedumonde.com

FRENCH MARKET SEAFOOD CO.
Fresh and frozen seafood such as blue crabs, crawfish, freshwater shrimp (prawns), and Louisiana oysters; andouille sausage; boudin; Cajun and Creole herbs, sauces, and seasonings
(800) 207-5691
www.frenchmarketseafood.com

GAMBINO'S BAKERY
King cakes, doberge cakes
(504) 712-0809
www.gambinos.com

INTERNET WINES AND SPIRITS
Herbsaint liqueur, Peychaud's bitters, Hurricane mix, bourbon, rye whiskey
(877) 624-1982
www.internetwines.com

NEW ORLEANS GROCER
Seeded muffuletta bread, pralines, king cakes, Creole and Cajun seasonings, filé
(704) 544-8853
www.neworleansgrocer.com

PROGRESS GROCERY
Seeded muffuletta bread, olive salad, Creole and Cajun seasonings, hot sauces
(504) 455-3663
progressgrocery.gourmetfoodmall.com

TEE-EVA'S WORLD FAMOUS PIES AND PRALINES
Pecan pralines, pecan pies, sweet potato pies
(504) 899-8350
www.tee-eva.net

INDEX

ACKNOWLEDGMENTS

Constance Snow would like to thank Ken Snow, Richard Benz, Liv Blumer, William Blumer, Hazell Boyce, Kathy Boyd, Sam Boyd, Lally Brennan, JoAnn Clevenger, Kristen Essig, Corbin Evans, Roy Finamore, Kathleen Hill, Carolyn Kolb, Richard McCarthy, Tory McPhail, Matthew Murphy, Lazone Randolph, Jane Ruppel, Ed Sherrill, Ken Smith, Susan Smith, Susan Spicer, Molly Stevens, Priscilla Vayda, and Bonnie Warren.

Weldon Owen and the photography team would like to extend their deepest thanks to the employees and owners of Brennan's Restaurant, Café du Monde, Destrehan Plantation, Joey K's Restaurant & Bar, Le Petit Grocery, Lilette Restaurant, Maison Carondelet, Muriel's Jackson Square, The Living Room, Upperline Restaurant, and the local farmers' markets, seafood and meat markets, and street markets of New Orleans, who remind us why we love good ol' Southern hospitality. They also wish to extend their gratitude to the owners and workers of the restaurants, bakeries, shops, and other culinary businesses in New Orleans who participated in this project: Acadian Bistro, Acme Oyster House, Angelo Brocato's Ice Cream and Confectionery, Antoine's, Audubon Zoo, Bayona and chef Susan Spicer, Bistro at Maison de Ville, Brigtsen's, Café Latrobe, Café Sbisa, Casamento's, Central Grocery, The Columns Hotel, Commander's Palace, La Crepe Nanou, Delmonico, Dick and Jenny's, Dooky Chase and chef Leah Chase, Emeril's, The French Market, The French Restaurant, Galatoire's Restaurant, Grenier & Chocolat, Half Moon Bar & Restaurant, Hermann Grima House Cooking School, Hotel Monteleone, International House Hotel, Lafitte's Blacksmith Shop, Martin Wine Cellar, Napolean House, Nola Restaurant, Old Absinthe House, Palm Court Jazz Café, Peristyle, The Praline Connection, Schaefer & Rusich Seafood Bar, Snug Harbor Jazz Bistro, La Spiga Bakery, Tee-Eva's World Famous Pies and Pralines, Tujague's Restaurant, Uglesich's Restaurant, and Voodoo Blues. The team would also like to thank Richard Ryan, Garibaldi's in Oakland, California, and Elite Café in San Francisco, California.

Weldon Owen also wishes to thank the following individuals for their kind assistance: Desne Ahlers, Carrie Bradley, Ken DellaPenta, Denise Santoro Lincoln, Sharon Silva, Kenneth Snow, and Sharron Wood.

PHOTO CREDITS

Francesca Yorke, all photography, except for the following:

Quentin Bacon: Pages 13, 36–37, 44–45, 54–55, 62–63, 68, 72, 79, 83, 84, 92, 94, 96, 100, 105, 110, 114, 119, 121, 125, 126, 134, 140, 143, 147, 150, 152–153, 155, 157, 158–159, 164, 172, 176, 180, 183

Jeffrey Barr: Pages 40, 47

©Bettmann/CORBIS: Page 171

Luis Castaneda/Getty Images: Page 38

©Michael S. Lewis/CORBIS: Page 57 (top)

©Nathan Benn/CORBIS: Page 41

©Philip Gould/CORBIS: Front cover (top), pages 39 (bottom center and right), 79, 169

Ronald Rammelkamp/Getty Images: Page 95

PHOTOGRAPHY LOCATIONS

The following New Orleans locations have been given references for the map on pages 28–29.

PAGE	LOCATION (MAP COORDINATES)
2	Brennan's (J-2)
6	Uglesich's (I-4)
8	Napoleon House Bar (J-2)
10	The Columns Hotel (G-6)
13	(top) Chef Susan Spicer, Bayona Restaurant (J-2)
14	Emeril's (J-3)
17	Emeril's (J-3)
18	Crescent City Farmers' Market (J-3)
21	Martin Wine Cellar (G-5)
22	Bourbon Street (J-2)
23	(bottom) Central Grocery Company (J-2)
25	St. Charles Avenue mansion (H-5)
27	(top) Lafayette Cemetery No. 1 (H-5)
32	Tujague's (J-2)
33	(top) Café Sbisa (J-2); (bottom center) Carousel Bar (J-2)
35	(right) International House Hotel, Loa Bar (J-3)
39	(top) Café Sbisa (J-2); (bottom right) Abbeville Giant Omelette Festival
41	Mardi Gras Festival
43	(all) Central Grocery (J-2)
51	(top) Antoine's Restaurant (J-2)
57	(top) Café du Monde (J-2)
58	(bottom left) Dooky Chase (I-1)
62	(all) Brennan's (J-2)
64	Casamento's (G-6)
71	Peristyle (J-1)
74	Antoine's Restaurant (J-2)
80	Chef Susan Spicer, Bayona Restaurant (J-2)
85	Acme Oyster House (J-2)
86	Frank Brigtsen, Brigtsen's (C-3)
97	Napoleon House Bar (J-2)
99	St. Louis Cathedral (J-2)
101	View of New Orleans from Ritz-Carlton (J-2)
106	Emeril's (J-3)
113	Commander's Palace (H-5)
118	Schaefer & Rusich Seafood Market (M-5 inset)
124	Antoine's Restaurant (J-2)
129	Upperline Restaurant (F-6)
131	Acme Oyster House (J-2)
133	Dick and Jenny's (G-7)
135	Palm Court Jazz Café (K-2)
136	Galatoire's (J-2)
144	Commander's Palace (H-5)
146	Bistro at Maison de Ville (J-2)
149	Café Latrobe (J-2)
156	Café Latrobe (J-2)
171	Mardi Gras Festival
179	Nola Restaurant (J-2)
180	Café du Monde (J-2)

OXMOOR HOUSE INC.

Oxmoor House books are distributed by Sunset Books
80 Willow Road, Menlo Park, CA 94025
Telephone: 650-321-3600 Fax: 650-324-1532
Vice President/General Manager Rich Smeby
National Accounts Manager/Special Sales Brad Moses
Oxmoor House and Sunset Books are divisions of
Southern Progress Corporation

WILLIAMS-SONOMA, INC.

Founder & Vice-Chairman Chuck Williams

THE FOODS OF THE WORLD SERIES

Conceived and produced by Weldon Owen Inc.
814 Montgomery Street, San Francisco, CA 94133
Telephone: 415-291-0100 Fax: 415-291-8841

In Collaboration with Williams-Sonoma, Inc.
3250 Van Ness Avenue, San Francisco, CA 94109

A Weldon Owen Production
Copyright © 2005 Weldon Owen Inc.
and Williams-Sonoma, Inc.

First printed in 2005
10 9 8 7 6 5 4 3 2 1

ISBN 0-8487-3103-4

Printed by Tien Wah Press
Printed in Singapore

WELDON OWEN INC.

Chief Executive Officer John Owen
President and Chief Operating Officer Terry Newell
Chief Financial Officer Christine E. Munson
Vice President International Sales Stuart Laurence
Creative Director Gaye Allen
Publisher Hannah Rahill

Series Editor Kim Goodfriend
Editor Emily Miller
Editorial Assistant Juli Vendzules

Art Director Nicky Collings
Designer Rachel Lopez

Production Director Chris Hemesath
Color Specialist Teri Bell
Production and Reprint Coordinator Todd Rechner

Food and Prop Stylist George Dolese
Associate Food Stylist Elisabet der Nederlanden
Photographer's Assistants James Carr, Paul Crocket,
and Heidi Ladendorf
Map Illustrator Bart Wright

JACKET IMAGES

Front cover: French Quarter building; Seafood Gumbo,
page 91. Back cover: St. Louis Cathedral on Jackson
Square; Louisiana Seafood Boil, page 115; New
Orleans–Style Barbecued Shrimp, page 111. Front
flap: Bourbon Street. Back flap: Beignets, page 181,
at Café du Monde.

A NOTE ON WEIGHTS AND MEASURES

All recipes include customary U.S. and metric
measurements. Metric conversions are based on
a standard developed for these books and have
been rounded off. Actual weights may vary.